RUSS GOMM

# THE BLAIR WITCH PROJECT

FOREWORD BY
EDUARDO SANCHEZ

THIS IS AN ARROW BOOK
PUBLISHED BY ARROW FILM DISTRIBUTORS
The Engine House, Shenley Park, Radlett Lane, Shenley, WD7 9JP
www.arrowfilms.com

**THE BLAIR WITCH PROJECT**


ISBN 978-0-993306-03-7
First Edition, First Printing
Printed in EU, 2018



**Editor** Jenai Laignel / Simon Ward
**Cover illustration** Peter Strain
**Design** Oink Creative

For Lorraine, Sheila & Douglas

Burkittsville

# Contents

## Chapter Seven



## Chapter Six



## Chapter Nine



## Chapter Ten



## Chapter Eleven



## Chapter Twelve

# Foreword

## Eduardo Sanchez

Russ Gomm is a freak.

A *Blair Witch Project* freak.

And I love him for it...

We met online years ago. Russ is a talented filmmaker and he sent me a link to his short film and I told him I dug it and we became friends. Then, the *Blair Witch* questions began. They never stopped. Here we are, years later, and the Russ Gomm *Blair Witch* book I always knew he would write has come to fruition.

Russ covers it from beginning to end, the whole crazy ride, starting with a truly unblemished fan's perspective of the phenomena, then shifting into real insider information on *The Blair Witch Project*'s unique production process and marketing techniques. Finally, he examines the lasting effects of this little film that came out of nowhere to blow up in the early summer of 1999. A little film that for some reason is still being talked about today...

I consider myself very fortunate to have been a part of making *The Blair Witch Project*. Its crazy success was as much a surprise to us it as it was to the rest of the world. We knew we had a cool idea, but never imagined what was about to happen to us when we set out to make the film in October of 1997 in the woods of Maryland. It was a thrill for me to relive this amazing part of my life through Russ' eyes.

Congratulations, my friend! I can't wait for the fans to read it.

Eduardo Sanchez
May 7, 2017

# Introduction

## Daniel Myrick

*The Blair Witch Project* was unlike anything we had attempted before.

I came from a more traditional photographic background and have always admired the cinematic approach of filmmakers like Stanley Kubrick, David Lean and Ridley Scott. So much information is conveyed in their every shot. As a visual storyteller, communicating non-verbally is every bit as important as what is in the dialogue. However, with *Blair*, we had to rely much more on the "implication" of what was on screen, rather than a more literal interpretation. This takes a lot of trust in not only the subject matter but in your actors, since we were relying so much on them to produce the actual footage we hoped for.

Neal Fredericks, our good friend and director of photography on the project, oversaw both the video and film cameras that we used. It was decided, relatively late in the game, that we were going to have a stylistic separation between Heather's footage (what she used for her actual project) and the so-called behind-the-scenes video which ultimately made up most of the finished film. This separation would help convey Heather's intent and ultimate goal of documenting the *Blair* mythology, giving us a nice way of communicating backstory and exposition, as well as using the BTS material as our day-to-day narrative through line.

Of course, at the time we weren't sure how this very non-traditional approach would work out. It was quite challenging for us as directors to relinquish so much control during production but we felt that if we covered as much content as possible, the bulk of the directing would be done during editing, more like a standard documentary. Nevertheless, we still managed to monitor much of what was shot during the nine days in the field and were able to make adjustments to the performances and narrative trajectory along the way. We were able to interact with the actors during production through a system of notes that we left for them at designated drop-off points, thus allowing them to read our instructions without having to break character.

This ended up working out really well and kept the on-set dynamic uninterrupted for the most part. It also allowed for the actors to experiment a little, since all their dialogue was mostly improvised, thus giving them the freedom to go places without being "edited" too much as they progressed.

Once they dialled in, our instructions for them were designed to hit certain key points along the way, but we left it up to them to decide when the time was right to hit them. Again, it was non-traditional filmmaking – something that was experimental by its nature and outside our comfort zone, but the collaboration between all of us made it possible. It was a sort of collective vision that we all had, and between myself, Ed, Gregg, Mike, Neal and Ben, we managed to keep each other in check and on the same page as the film started to take shape. But in the end, just like with any film, you never know if what you have is doing its job until it is screened in front of a bunch of strangers.

# Introduction

## Russ Gomm

Hey, fellow *Blair Witch*/horror/film fan! Thanks so much for picking up this little book. Hopefully you will find inside these pages a comprehensive look at one of the most incredible independent horror films of recent years, celebrating its twentieth anniversary in 2019.

You hold in your hands something very special. This is more than a book. It is a time machine and I want you to come with me on a fantastic voyage back to the land of the soul patch, tucked-in t-shirts, stonewashed jeans and pagers. Journey back to 1999 and beyond with me as we look over the history and the making of *The Blair Witch Project*, a film that is very close to my heart and one that is extremely important – not just in its highly original and unique production methods, but also in turning the industry upside-down with an innovative marketing strategy that caught the attention of the whole world.

I often find myself in deep conversations about the film. I love to talk about it with anyone who is interested: fans, filmmakers, even people who look at me strangely because they have "never heard of this *Blair Witch* film". I have to remind myself that the film is a product of its time and you arguably had to be there to fully appreciate it. However, if you belong to our brand new generation of horror film fans and are just discovering the classics from the Sixties, Seventies, Eighties and Nineties, this book is as much for you as it is for those who caught it first time around.

This tome will serve as a unique reference, looking at every aspect of this one-of-a-kind production and each chapter will deal with a very specific element of the film, from its inception to the ground-breaking marketing strategy.

We'll also look at personal *Blair Witch* experiences from directors, critics and fans alike and how they perceived the phenomenon of *The Blair Witch Project* and the effect it had on their lives.

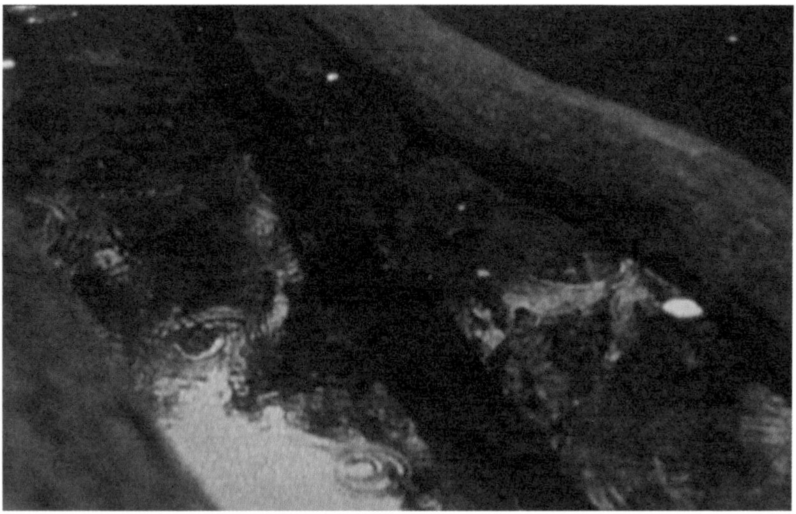

The film is one of the scariest that I have ever seen. I don't imagine any other film would be able to leave such a mark on me and I know many fans feel the same. But it isn't just because of those intensely claustrophobic 81 minutes of screen time – it is so much more than just a movie. An intricate and carefully-planned universe was created by the filmmakers, giving us a rich and detailed narrative that the audience could completely disappear in, just like those three unlucky campers did in the Black Hills forest. So grab your hiking boots and survival kit and join me as we journey deeper into the woods than ever before. Just make sure you are out by nightfall.

# Chapter One

## America – summer 1999

This is where it all began for me: my lifelong obsession with *The Blair Witch Project*.

I was a young, know-it-all genre fan with a dedicated passion for horror films, a passion that began and continues in the realm of low-budget horror filmmaking. The early classics that stole my heart were the same films that numerous fans and filmmakers alike often reference: *The Evil Dead* (Sam Raimi, 1981), *The Texas Chainsaw Massacre* (Tobe Hooper, 1974), *Night of the Living Dead* (George A. Romero, 1968), to name just a few.

From the mid to late Nineties things had begun to change (more on that later) and I found myself caught up in the ever so popular and trendy slasher film cycle. I can't remember which one of these classics I saw first – it could have been *Scream* (Wes Craven, 1996) or *Urban Legend* (Jamie Blanks, 1998) or *I Know What You Did Last Summer* (Jim Gillespie, 1997), but I became just as obsessed with these high-gloss, big-budget, mainstream entries into my beloved genre as I was with films from the opposite end of the scale. I even started collecting those hip soundtracks with music from the films, including hits from my soon-to-be-favourite bands: Kula Shaker, The Offspring, Creed and Everclear. I found myself watching these new slasher films over and over and desperately awaiting the sequels (of which there were many), but I never forgot about my real true love of down and dirty horror films.

In the lead-up to the summer of 1999, I, along with a great many other people, was starting to get excited about an upcoming film which looked like it would scare the absolute shit out of anyone who planned to watch it. That film was *The Sixth Sense* (M. Night Shyamalan) and it was going to be *the* great horror film of 1999. But that was before I went on holiday to Seattle.

That was before I knew what was waiting on the horizon.

That was before I first heard those four words which still send a shiver down my spine...

*The Blair Witch Project*.

This was the moment that everything changed. I was on holiday in the States with my father for a couple of weeks and we were travelling from Vancouver through the Canadian Rockies, Montana, Idaho and Washington State, to our final destination, Seattle, a magnificent but cold city with a coffee shop on every street corner. It was July 11th 1999 and after another full day of sightseeing we returned to the hotel and watched TV. I wish I could recall what was on at the time but during the very regular commercial breaks my attention was grabbed. An advert for what looked like a true crime documentary appeared on screen. Normally this wouldn't interest me but I distinctly remember hearing that three student filmmakers had gone missing in the woods while making a documentary about a local witch. At the time, I myself was a student filmmaker and instantly panicked about these poor missing students. Of course I was hooked instantly and had to watch this upcoming Sci-Fi Channel documentary *Curse of the Blair Witch* (Daniel Myrick and Eduardo Sanchez, 1999).

For the hour that the show was on I didn't move and I didn't talk. I just became more and more terrified at the thought that these three students had been "taken" by this witch. I just couldn't get the thought of it out of my head. "Where are they? Are they dead? Did the witch get them?" To this day I don't recall my father actually telling me whether he believed the story or not. To me there was never even a question about its authenticity. I completely, one hundred percent believed everything that I had just been shown and told regarding the *Blair Witch*. At the conclusion of the show we found out one important thing – a group of filmmakers had been given access to the footage and had cut it together to try and understand the mystery of the disappearance. The family of the missing students had allowed the footage to be shown to the public and at the end of the week the film would be shown in several theatres around the country so that you could witness the events yourself.

What???

A "snuff movie" on the big screen?

I immediately told my father that we HAD to go and see this thing called *The Blair Witch Project* and lucky for us it was playing in a small university town not far away. The night that I watched *Curse of the Blair Witch* was the first of many sleepless nights thanks to this intriguing and disturbing legend.

We set off to the Seattle University district on Saturday 17th July to see the film. We found the cinema, The Neptune Theatre (on NE 45th and Brooklyn Avenue), easily. It wasn't hard to miss the huge queue snaking around the block and the giant, old-fashioned canopy with huge lettering detailing the title of this mysterious new film. I remember filming some of this with my very own Sony Hi-8 Camera as part of our holiday video.

As we got closer to the cinema my heart sank as I saw the words "All Performances Sold Out!" on the doors of the cinema. Unfortunately it was our last day in the States, and so I was denied the opportunity to see the film just yet. However, this may have been a blessing in disguise. As my wait for the film grew, so too did my obsession and when the film finally arrived in the UK, just in time for Halloween, my bewilderment over what was real, fake, legend or otherwise was at its peak.

I was ready. Or at least I thought I was.

# Chapter Two

## England – autumn 1999

The more I looked into the film and mythology, the more I became convinced that it was all real. I visited the website[1] which contained a timeline of historic events relating to the *Blair Witch*. There were even crime scene photos and excerpts of Heather's journal (which the website claimed had been discovered by the police, along with the Hi-8 Tapes and 16mm Film Rolls).

How could this not be real?

In the beginning there was a never even a doubt in my mind about the legitimacy of the film. As time passed, people started talking about the film in a way that suggested it was a work of fiction. I absolutely love legends and myths, so a big part of me wanted it to all be real and, in a strange way, I still do.

Was the *Blair Witch* herself a real legend?

With more visits to the website it seemed that it was indeed genuine. I mean, it was all written out as history in black and white – and surely this internet thingy wouldn't lie to us? Even IMDb (The Internet Movie Database) had listed all three of the students as "Missing, presumed dead".

If there were ever any doubt in my mind, this was soon put to rest when I discovered *The Blair Witch Project: A Dossier* – a book written (or compiled, as we were led to believe) by D.A. Stern. It contained police investigation files, letters and documents all carefully assembled to weave its very own enthralling and terrifying story. This dossier served its purpose and filled my head with even more seemingly indisputable mythology.

---

1 www.blairwitch.com – the 1999 incarnation of the site currently resides at www.blairwitch.com/project/main.html courtesy of archivist Dan Karcher.

Summer came to an end and the nights grew longer and darker. *The Blair Witch Project* was gaining notoriety. October was getting closer.

I picked up *The Blair Witch Project: Josh's Blair Witch Mix* in the local HMV and wondered just what the hell it was. My first piece of *Blair Witch* merchandise! (I didn't count the book at the time, because it felt like non-fiction. It seemed so real.) I distinctly remember feeling awful after buying the CD, thinking how macabre it was to have a soundtrack to a "snuff film". This uneasiness was not dispelled when I opened the CD case and it had the following written inside:

*Dedicated to the memory of Heather, Mike and especially Josh, whose great taste in music inspired this album. R.I.P.*

The CD was apparently a compilation of songs that had been on a tape that was discovered by police in the missing students' car.

And then there were the posters and trailers for the film. They showed nothing, but explained everything. They were simple and terrifying: to this day whenever I think of trees I instantly see that black and white image of the woods. These marketing tools promised us a film that we would never forget.

Along with everyone else, I was expecting a truly horrifying experience. It only took a few simple words on the posters and trailers to drill into our minds that this film was not fucking around when it came to being scary. What began as quotes from reviews and advertising soon started to sound more like a warning to the potential viewers of the film. The most enticing warning you could ever wish for:

*"The scariest movie of all time is a true story."*

*"Scarier than* The Exorcist*!"*

*"Scary as hell."*

*"Everything you've heard is true."*

Not only did those words send us cowering into the corner, they also gave one final affirmation that this film was real.

These subtle touches were what really sold the idea of the film to me. I hadn't realised it at the time but the documentary, the book and the CD had put my mind into a frenzy of questions with no answers – so much so that when I did finally watch the film, it was genuinely the scariest thing I had ever seen and, in spite of months of waiting, right afterwards I wished that I could un-see the horrors that I had just witnessed.

## The Blair Witch Experience

## Jake West

*Jake West is a film director and editor from the UK and has directed* Razor Blade Smile *(1998),* Evil Aliens *(2005),* Pumpkinhead: Ashes to Ashes *(2006) and* Doghouse *(2009). Jake also co-runs the UK production company Nucleus Films which was established to distribute rare cult films and to produce documentaries for home video releases.*

Like most people I became aware of *The Blair Witch Project* ahead of the release because it was one of the first films to use the internet to create a mythology. I hadn't really visited anything online particularly before I saw the film, it's more that there were just a lot of people talking about it at the time in the media – reading about it in magazines and hearing about it on TV. It was a film that seemed to come out of nowhere.

As a filmmaker I was interested in anyone who made a low budget horror film, so I wanted to see it for that reason, although my initial reaction was that I wasn't sure it would be my kind of thing as it was done in a more realistic, documentary style. However, after the screening at Sundance, the media began reporting how people who had seen the film thought it was real.

This was the thing that amused me the most as I never believed it was a real documentary. I knew *The Blair Witch Project* was made by filmmakers. I had heard of Daniel Myrick and Eduardo Sanchez so I was aware that there was a film production behind it and I was interested in that whole aspect.

Like everyone, I was curious to see the film and I happened to be on holiday when I eventually saw it in Paris, a month or so before it was released in London. The audience reaction was good and people were freaked out. I had to ignore the French subtitles, but it created such an atmosphere. It is quite an experimental horror film in a sense – it's not full of scares but it becomes terrifying through its use of atmosphere.

I thought the film was very interesting and had really naturalistic performances – particularly Heather Donahue. But what I liked about the film the most was that it had worked out a very clear mythology and the thinking behind the whole legend of the *Blair Witch*. I liked that aspect so much that I actually bought the companion book afterwards because I wanted to read more. I was impressed that they had figured out a "real mythology" which gave it a feeling of it being more real than other films like it.

As an intersection, because I was a low-budget filmmaker and I had just made my first film in 1997, *Razor Blade Smile*, I was actually asked to interview Dan Myrick and Eduardo Sanchez in the UK for the DVD release. The distributor wanted someone who wasn't going to ask them the usual press pack questions. It was really nice to meet them and they were still surprised by the success of the film.

Back in those days it was quite hard for independent films to break through into the mainstream. It was rare that a low-budget horror film received a proper cinema release. These days it is very different, but in the 1990s it was a real commitment. It was quite unusual for a film like that to be known about, but it did something that other films weren't doing which is why it stood out.

Maybe *The Blair Witch Project* gave filmmakers more confidence to use lower resolution tools and the ability to make films on a lower budget. From that perspective I think it was a good thing, but obviously it meant you had to suffer through quite a lot of bad films and imitations afterwards. Filmmaking was changing at that point as digital technology was beginning to be accepted, but the early DV cameras were not quite good enough, so a lot of that stuff still felt quite "video-y" and cheap.

In terms of marketing, using the internet was a new way of doing things and what they did then has now set the template for everything afterwards. I think that's why the film did particularly well in the States. In the UK the internet campaign didn't really mean as much. It obviously set a benchmark for future film campaigns and now pretty much every film has a website, but I think the way they used it was more playful. Because *The Blair Witch Project* was the first one to do it, there were people at the time who really did believe it was real, but I'm not sure people would believe that today.

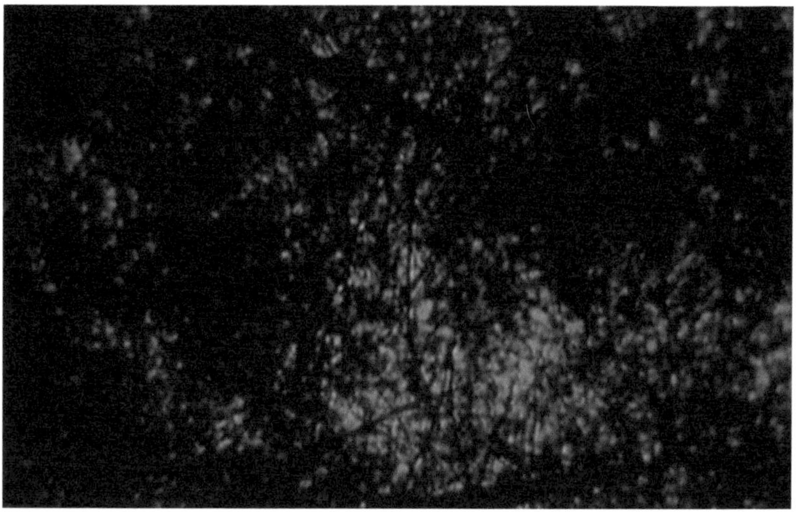

# Chapter Three

## The Nineties

There weren't too many big horror films in this decade, unless you count *Jurassic Park* (Steven Spielberg, 1993) which could be argued follows horror conventions. Here is the highest grossing film of each year.

TOP FILMS BY YEAR (unadjusted domestic gross totals)

1990: Home Alone (Chris Columbus)
1991: Terminator 2: Judgment Day (James Cameron)
1992: Aladdin (Ron Clements & John Musker)
1993: Jurassic Park (Steven Spielberg)
1994: The Lion King (Roger Allers & Rob Minkoff)
1995: Toy Story (John Lasseter)
1996: Independence Day (Roland Emmerich)
1997: Titanic (James Cameron)
1998: Saving Private Ryan (Steven Spielberg)
1999: Star Wars: Episode I - The Phantom Menace (George Lucas)

For the highest grossing films of the Nineties overall, the first and only horror entry is number seven (not counting the aforementioned *Jurassic Park*).

TOP TEN FILMS OF 1990s (unadjusted domestic gross totals)

1. Titanic (1997 – James Cameron)
2. Star Wars: Episode I - The Phantom Menace (1999 – George Lucas)
3. Jurassic Park (1993- Steven Spielberg)
4. Forrest Gump (1994 - Robert Zemeckis)
5. The Lion King (1994 - Roger Allers & Rob Minkoff)
6. Independence Day (1996 - Roland Emmerich)

7. The Sixth Sense (1999 - M. Night Shyamalan)
8. Home Alone (1990 – John Hughes)
9. Men in Black (1997 - Barry Sonnenfeld)
10. Toy Story 2 (1999 - John Lasseter)

For 1999 specifically, this list includes the total US gross takings and from how many screens.

| | | |
|---|---|---|
| 1. Star Wars: Episode I – The Phantom Menace | $431,088,295 | (3,126Screens) |
| 2. The Sixth Sense | $293,506,292 | (2,821Screens) |
| 3. Toy Story 2 | $245,852,179 | (3,257Screens) |
| 4. Austin Powers: The Spy Who Shagged Me | $206,040,086 | (3,314Screens) |
| 5. The Matrix | $171,479,930 | (2,903Screens) |
| 6. Tarzan | $171,091,819 | (3,131Screens) |
| 7. Big Daddy | $163,479,795 | (3,254Screens) |
| 8. The Mummy | $155,385,488 | (3,411Screens) |
| 9. Runaway Bride | $152,257,509 | (3,240Screens) |
| 10. The Blair Witch Project | $140,539,099 | (2,538Screens) |

There we are, sitting nicely at number ten. A film made for an estimated $60,000, sitting in the top ten alongside mega-budget blockbusters that played on many more screens nationwide.

It is strange to think that while we were watching all of the big budget Hollywood spectaculars and all of the countless genre sequels so early on in the Nineties, a small band of rebel filmmakers were already taking their first steps towards creating the most original and terrifying film of 1999.

I often wonder what the film industry would be like if *The Blair Witch Project* hadn't been there to shake things up. How different would the horror genre be? How would studios look at marketing? How inventive would independent films be and how would their productions be different? Which walls would still be standing now if *The Blair Witch Project* hadn't knocked them down?

Let's take a look back over this important decade and remind ourselves just what the face of horror was like back then.

The first horror film to reach UK cinemas in the Nineties was *A Nightmare on Elm Street Part 5: The Dream Child* (Stephen Hopkins), the latest sequel in the popular franchise which had begun back in 1984. The film was released on Friday 11th May 1990 and was followed by several other scare flicks, such as *Re-Animator 2* – a.k.a. *Bride of Re-Animator* (Brian Yuzna) and *Gremlins 2: The New Batch* (Joe Dante) in July, *Nightbreed* (Clive Barker) in September, *Hardware* (Richard Stanley) in October and *The Exorcist III* (William Peter Blatty) in November. What is interesting about these films is that, firstly, it shows there weren't actually that many horror films released on the big screen at this time and secondly, of the few that were, more than half were sequels.

Obviously there were a lot more horror films available to consumers on video, but not many of those made it to the big screen in the UK during the 1990s.

At the time I would have devoured any film that came my way. You really had to go out of your way to see films. There was no Netflix or Amazon Prime, nor a bazillion channels to pick from. If you wanted to see a film, you saw it on the big screen, waited half a year to see it on video or endured many more months after that for it to appear on satellite TV. Films would then find their final resting place on terrestrial TV where they would be butchered, disjointed with adverts, be played in almost unwatchable "pan and scan" and have some horrendous announcer talk all over the end credits (which were usually played at double speed to get through them quicker).

For me it was an honour to see any film and at an early age, with a life full of film watching ahead of me, I had very little need to be picky; I watched whatever I could, whenever I could, often with many repeat viewings. I was most certainly a very happy individual when it came to sequels and remakes. A film was a film and I found some merit in almost everything that I watched. I was excited to flick through pages of the local video store magazine and see that there was a new *Friday the 13th* or *Halloween* instalment coming our way soon.

Horror films started to lose their edge in the Nineties. There were some real gems and we were treated to some incredible genre films, but ask many true horror fans and they'll all agree: things weren't looking too good.

The Nineties continued in the same way that it started. A few original horror films emerged from between the many sequels that landed on UK cinema screens.

1991 started quickly with *Child's Play 2* (John Lafia) and *Maniac Cop 2* (William Lustig) in January, but it then took months for the next genre film to arrive. *Predator 2* (Stephen Hopkins) arrived in May along with *Misery* (Rob Reiner), followed by everyone's favourite *The Silence of the Lambs* (Jonathan Demme) in June. That was pretty much it for the year until late in December when *The People Under the Stairs* (Wes Craven) was released.

Big genre films from 1992 included *Freddy's Dead: The Final Nightmare* (Rachel Talalay) in January, *Split Second* (Tony Maylam) in June, *Sleepwalkers* (Mick Garris) in July and *Alien*$^3$ (David Fincher) in August. *Child's Play 3* (Jack Bender) arrived in November to finish what had largely been an underwhelming year for film.

In 1993 Bram Stoker's *Dracula* (Francis Ford Coppola) opened the year with a big bang followed by *Hellraiser III: Hell on Earth* (Anthony Hickox), which happens to be my favourite of the series! *Candyman* (Bernard Rose) appeared in March. The obviously awesome (but toned down from previous entries in the series) *Army of Darkness* (Sam Raimi) was *the* big screen outing that summer for horror fans. Other than this it wasn't a huge year for horror at the cinema, but we did get some classics on video such as *Dollman vs. Demonic Toys* (Charles Band), *Jason Goes To Hell: The Final Friday* (Adam Marcus), *Leprechaun* (Mark Jones), *Puppet Master 4* (Jeff Burr), *The Tommyknockers* (John Power) and *Warlock: The Armageddon* (Anthony Hickox). We were also finally treated to a VHS release of the gore-filled remake of *Night of the Living Dead* (Tom Savini), which had taken a couple of years to get to us.

Sadly in 1994 there wasn't really a lot to report on cinematic genre outing. *The Crow* (Alex Proyas) was released in June, but directors like Quentin Tarantino, James Cameron and Robert Zemeckis dominated cinema screens with their films *Pulp*

*Fiction*, *True Lies* and *Forrest Gump*, respectively. Tarantino was the new darling of cinema, and dialogue-filled crime movies became fashionable during the rest of the Nineties, leaving less room in the market place for "genre pictures". In September we experienced *Cronos* (Guillermo del Toro) and then, in November, *Mary Shelley's Frankenstein* (Kenneth Branagh) brought a new take on the classic horror film. I should probably also mention *The Texas Chainsaw Massacre: The Next Generation* – a.k.a. *Return of the Texas Chainsaw Massacre* (Kim Henkel) which was supposed to be released somewhere on video this year (although probably not in the UK).

1995 started in style with *Wes Craven's New Nightmare*, a fantastic continuation of the *Nightmare on Elm Street* saga. In the middle of the year horror picked up with *Demon Knight* – a.k.a. *Tales from the Crypt Presents: Demon Knight* (Ernest Dickerson) and *In the Mouth of Madness* (John Carpenter) in June. *Night of the Demons 2* (Brian Trenchard-Smith) arrived on video this year... I didn't see that one.

It was 1996 when horror really began to change. In January audiences were shocked to find out what was really in that box in *Se7en* (David Fincher), followed a few months later by *From Dusk Till Dawn* (Robert Rodriguez) which fooled some audiences into believing it was a straightforward Tarantino-esque crime movie before suddenly turning into a gory vampire flick. Wes Craven was back again with *Vampire in Brooklyn*, which had nothing on *New Nightmare* and gave no hint at the excitement of his next project.

In 1997, Craven was king. He took all that made *New Nightmare* incredible and spun it into a brand new take that changed the face of horror. So many words were thrown around to describe the masterpiece that is *Scream* – postmodern, meta, self-referential – but really the film started a brand new trend which would continue and dominate the market for the next few years – for better or for worse.

*Scream* was pretty much the first and last word in horror of 1997, but it would be wrong to dismiss other entries in the genre. In January *The Frighteners* (Peter Jackson) became an unexpected hit, combining the great comedy-horror elements we had seen in Jackson's earlier work with a big studio budget and paired the always loveable Michael J. Fox with genre legend Jeffrey Combs. The absolutely mental *Event Horizon*

(Paul W.S. Anderson) assaulted our screens and our senses in August. The year ended with the next entry in the teen-slasher sub-genre that *Scream* started: *I Know What You Did Last Summer* paved the way for a new type of horror film.

In May 1998 Wes Craven (yes, Wes Craven again) managed to top his brilliant slasher flick *Scream* with the over-the-top and outrageous *Scream 2*. Completely opposite to the trend however was the re-release of *The Exorcist* (William Friedkin) for Halloween – the first time it had been shown legally in the UK since 1984 when it was removed from video stores as part of the video nasties scandal.

Continuing the teen-slasher trend was *Halloween H20: Twenty Years Later* (Steve Miner), which followed a similar postmodern approach to horror as *Scream* and *I Know What You Did Last Summer*.[2] *Blade* (Stephen Norrington) arrived in November, bringing the year of horror to a fun close.

This leads us to 1999. The turning point.

Next in line to cleverly chop up teen victims was *Urban Legend* in February and then Kevin Williamson continued his quest to change horror with *The Faculty* (Robert Rodriguez). The teens continued to be stalked and slashed in both this and *I Still Know What You Did Last Summer* (Danny Cannon) in April and May respectively. In between those films, 8mm (Joel Schumacher) was a rather nasty little thriller that reminded us that it wasn't just about slicing and dicing promiscuous teenagers.

And then, horror went quiet.

Until October.

---

2 It would be remiss not to mention script writer Kevin Williamson at this point as he was a big part of that movement (even though Williamson by this point was too busy for *Halloween H20* and could only offer up the original treatment for the film).

*The Sixth Sense* (M. Night Shyamalan) and *The Blair Witch Project* arrived just in time for Halloween and completely turned the horror genre on its head. No one expected them or the impact they would have.

Things would never be the same again.

## The Blair Witch Experience

## Garland Triest

*Garland Triest is an American musician and voice actor best known for his vocal contributions to the films* As Above So Below *(John Erick Dowdle, 2014) and* Krampus *(Michael Dougherty, 2015), as well as his rock band Angelrage.*

In the fall of 1999, I heard about a new horror film that was supposedly edited from some found footage shot by three missing college students. My friends said it was scary as hell and I had also heard that some people had been throwing up in the aisles because watching the film had made them physically ill. At the time, I was recovering from a severe car accident and was pretty busted up, with internal injuries that prevented me from venturing very far from home. But I knew that I had to see *The Blair Witch Project*.

I found that the film was playing nearby and, in a very uncharacteristic move; I went to the theatre alone. That night, there in the dark, something extraordinary happened. I forgot I was watching a film. I forgot I was safe. My heart was pounding and my ears were ringing with fear. It's the only film that's ever elicited such a visceral reaction and I doubt any ever will again.

I wasn't aware of the documentary at the time of seeing the film and it wasn't until later on that I saw it on TV and visited the website. I got my first computer right before the film came out and I was new to the internet. When I found the website, I spent hours on it. I couldn't believe the amount of work they put into the backstory and mythology. Before I saw the film I had seen the TV spot and the word on the street was that the film was supposedly real. My gut told me it couldn't possibly be, but by the end, I was sitting there shaking, waiting to see if there was a disclaimer.

I went in a sceptic but the film suspended my disbelief. It was electrifying. A funny thing about the TV spot: there's a line in it where Josh says, "I ain't gonna die, Pa." and I remember being perplexed when I saw the film that this line wasn't included. I realised there was much more footage and over the years I've been a little obsessive about collecting every deleted scene I can get my hands on.

Aside from the film itself, the website was a game changer. After *The Blair Witch Project*, movie websites would never look the same and as studios scrambled to cash in, found footage would become a popular and polarising genre all of its own.

I love the entire *Blair Witch* universe – the sequels, soundtrack CDs, books, games, posters, t-shirts and every piece of memorabilia I can get my hands on. One of my favourite things about it was that every time you bought one of the VHS documentaries or the soundtrack CD, you were treated to another deleted scene from the film; another piece of the puzzle. They created such a rich, sprawling universe for fans to explore.

I was ecstatic to see a new film in theatres in 2016 and I hope the *Blair Witch* will be haunting us for a long time to come.

# Chapter Four

## The black chapters

Eduardo Sanchez and Daniel Myrick are two very unique film directors with a passion to make original and dynamic cinema. They have become legendary within horror circles, and have both worked continuously (although often separately) on a variety of projects, both within the horror genre and away from it.

Eduardo Sanchez was born in Cuba in 1968 and went to Spain when he was just two years old. His family moved him to America when he was five, where he eventually settled. Ed had a passion for film from an early age and started with television production in the eleventh grade of high school. From the first week of class he realised what he wanted to do for the rest of his life.

At Montgomery College in Maryland he made his first feature film *Video All* (1989), which was shot completely on VHS. This was a project that he both wrote and directed. Ed applied for entry into the University of Central Florida Film Program and was accepted. That summer Ed made another feature film, this time progressing to shooting on black and white 16mm. The resulting film was *Gabriel's Dream* (1992), which unfortunately never got sold for distribution and still remains largely unseen.

Ed met Dan in the first semester in film school and by the second semester they were working together.

Daniel Myrick was born in Sarasota, Florida, in 1963 and from an early age he had a keen interest in photography. At around the age of eleven Dan received his first 35mm photography kit. He became so interested in the technical side that he built his own darkroom in the bathroom to process his photographs. This early study helped to familiarise Dan with composition and other aspects of capturing images.

Dan was always fascinated by movies and TV and later became heavily involved in commercial production. After all of the video work Dan wanted to do something that would expand his horizons. Upon finishing at Emerson College in Fort Myers, Florida, he heard of the film program at University of Central Florida and immediately signed up for it, sending them a film essay and his reel.

During their time at film school, the pair made short films as part of the curriculum, including a one-minute film called *Rage* (1990) which Ed wrote and directed and Dan acted in. The next short was called *Fortune* (1990). This was the first film Ed and Dan co-directed and was made in the second semester. The film was under ten minutes in length and was shot on black and white 16mm film. It features a fortune teller, a witch and a voodoo curse. This was their first genre film. They continued to work together and came up with many more ideas before co-producing a feature length film called *The Black Chapters* (1993), which consisted of three separate shorts: *Salvation, Resurrection* and *Upstairs Man*. Dan and Ed each wrote and directed a short in the anthology along with fellow filmmaker (and *Blair Witch* producer) Gregg Hale. There were big hopes for the film and each of the three thirty minute segments was shot using 16mm film. The film was unfortunately abandoned during post production due to lack of resources.

Dan later took work as director of photography on a couple of feature films in the local area and also edited a couple of features. He expanded his commercial client base to such an extent that he was able to bring Ed and Gregg on board. From there the working relationships blossomed and, soon after, the opportunity arose to turn a kernel of an idea that Dan and Ed had originally come up with in film school into a fully fleshed-out screenplay.

Everything they had learned up to this point was about to be put to the test.

# The Blair Witch Experience

## Johannes Roberts

*Johannes Roberts is a British film director and writer. He made his feature debut at the age of 23 with* Sanitarium *(2001) and directed* When Evil Calls *(2006), which was the world's first short series for mobile phones. His more recent films include* Storage 24 *(2012),* The Other Side of the Door *(2016) and* 47 Meters Down *(2017).*

*The Blair Witch Project* was a moment in history not just for horror cinema, but cinema in general.

I was on the set of my first movie *Sanitarium* in 1999 when I first heard about a film called *The Blair Witch Project*. We all gathered around an article in a newspaper that talked about this tiny movie taking America by storm.

People talk a lot about how *Scream* rejuvenated the horror genre, but really I think *The Blair Witch Project* was the movie that totally changed everything (for good and bad – so, so many terrible found footage movies followed). It was scary. It was REAL. No jokes or winks to camera. No stars or named directors (maybe this film was the death knell for the Seventies greats that I had grown up with – Carpenter, Craven, etc.), just a great concept and an amazing marketing campaign. It really has to be seen as the forerunner to modern horror cinema. Without *The Blair Witch Project* there is no Blumhouse.[3]

I think with maybe the exception of Hollywood discovering J-Horror and assimilating it, there has never been a more influential moment in horror cinema than the release of *The Blair Witch Project*. I wonder if there ever will be, in my lifetime at least.

---

3 Blumhouse Productions is a film and TV company founded by Jason Blum and mostly known for producing low budget horror films, which often yield high returns.

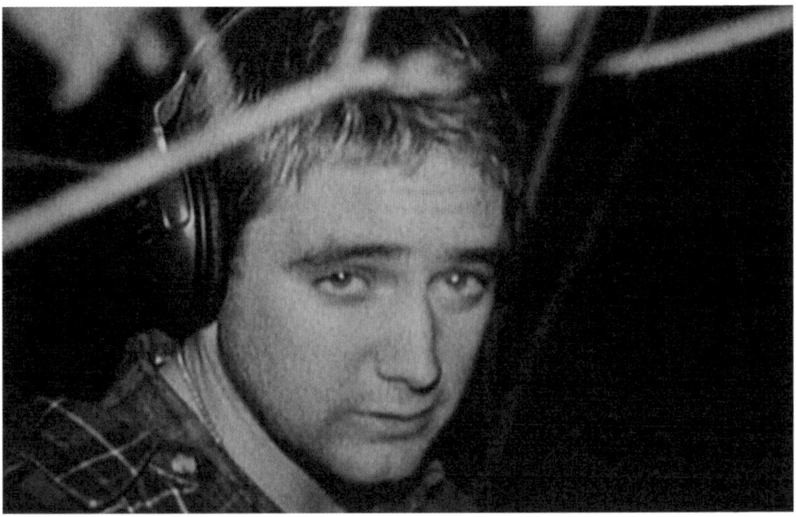

# Chapter Five

## Old school

It was 1991. Ed and Dan were still in film school. One weekend they got together with some other friends and started talking about horror films. Included in the conversation were the "real life" documentaries they had seen on TV when they were younger, films about Bigfoot, like *The Legend of Boggy Creek* (Charles B. Pierce, 1972), or aliens visiting ancient earth in *Chariots of the Gods* (Harald Reinl, 1970) and the incredible series *In Search of...* (1976–1982). After all of the talking the group rented a few video tapes – documentaries about Bigfoot, Nostradamus and the UFO conspiracies – and spent the weekend freaking themselves out over the content of these films. It seemed that there was a real lull in horror filmmaking at the time and nobody was crafting the type of films they wanted to see. Ed and Dan had similar ideas in mind.

As they discussed why certain films and ideas scared them so much (especially those they had originally seen as kids), they came up with a theory. They decided it was because the films were presented as factual, as real events. This idea of the horror of non-fiction had creeped Ed and Dan out when they were much younger but the fear returned when they watched the films again. Being film students, their instant reaction was to deliberate whether they could do the same in a feature film.

This is where initial concept for *The Blair Witch Project* came from. Was it possible to create a feature that was entirely reality based – just some people with a camera? Their first idea was to have a creepy house – and have one shot going through the house – full of blood, sacrifice and devil worship with a door at the end of the hallway. You would travel with the protagonist down the hallway, through the door and into the cellar where some freaky thing would happen.

The act of not cutting, the fact that you would have to stay with the action was what Ed and Dan were going after. The concept for the film was completely different to the finished film, but the seed is there, as is the intensity. This idea, to shoot a very realistic film about some explorers and what happened to them while they were filming their own journey (and ultimately their own demise), was a bolt of lightning. The conversations led to campfire-style storytelling sessions in which they created a two-hundred-year-old legend about an outcast, a cursed town and a series of unexplained disappearances.

As we have already learned, many genre films throughout the Nineties were becoming quite bland. There were very few original ideas getting made and the industry seemed more concerned with profits and selling *safe* horror films to younger audiences (with a few noted exceptions) than making original and terrifying films to shock and scare the true fans of horror.

The majority of the films made at this time were based on concepts that had already been explored in the Eighties, so the team behind *The Blair Witch Project* found their influences elsewhere. They weren't so interested in teen-slasher movies or films full of gore and destruction. They weren't trying to compete with the current wave of films which wanted to throw as many cheap jump scares and buckets of blood on screen as possible. Ed and Dan looked back further, into films filled with dark mythologies and no clear distinction between fact and fiction, films that would have had made an impact years before, but had now been discarded for a more modern style of filmmaking. For all of the money and stars and effects thrown into horror films in the Nineties, it was the film that had no money, no stars and no effects that ended up terrifying the world – a film that relied solely on atmosphere, tension and human drama. It was using old fashioned technique mixed with modern day thinking that gave the world one of the most unique and horrific cinematic experiences possible.

After the group had made their decision that this was the kind of film that they wanted to pursue, they needed to create a fictional world for their story to take place in. Ed was now based in Maryland and Dan would drive up for meetings in which they would outline the backstory: what is the witch? How did she come into being? What is the mythology behind her?

Together they brainstormed the history of the witch and the story of what would happen to the students while they were out in the woods. A lot of the pre-production, pre-planning and scenario-building came in at this stage. The duo had spent a good deal of time putting together the narrative behind the film, but it wasn't until Dan happened to have a conversation with Gregg Hale (whom he was working with on a separate script) about the idea for their horror film that the brakes came off and the film was vaulted into production. The idea captivated Gregg, who immediately decided that he would use his savings to make the film happen.

## The Blair Witch Experience

## Mitch Harrod

*Mitch Harrod is a dyed-in-the-wool horror fan. His first words out of the womb were, "Here's Johnny!" He's been a* Blair Witch *devotee since stumbling across its website in 1999. He's been obsessed ever since. Mitch is mental health counsellor by day and a film editor by night. He has edited shorts, films and festival trailers, and even an unofficial cut of* Book of Shadows.

In October of 1999 one film fan disappeared into a cinema in Gloucester, England...

Eighteen years later and the experience has never left him.

It's October 1999 and I, like so many others, have an image seemingly seared into my every waking (and sleeping) thought: the monochrome under-lit face of a girl, the unmistakable glint of fear in her eyes. Black monolithic trees shard the sky above her and right there in the middle of the image a red Stickman. This image was, for me, not just an image used in a poster, but a tantalising promise of true fear. A taboo. A dare.

Because unlike so many others whipped into fervour by that one sheet, in October of 1999 I was eight years old.

Of course, like any credible horror fan with a taste for the rapscallion, I wasn't going to let this stop me. But unlike countless titles before it, *The Gate* (Tibor Takacs, 1987),

*Chopping Mall* (Jim Wynorski, 1986) and the dread *Scarecrows* (William Wesley, 1988), I wouldn't be able to get the morally-questionable, local video library clerk to hide me *this* title in a Disney clamshell; I couldn't wait twelve months for it to come to VHS. That's if it did come out on video – after all, I'd heard it was real. The police were going to ban it. IT'S TOO SCARY FOR PUBLIC CONSUMPTION. As such, I needed a plan – and that plan came in the guise of a dare.

"I dare you to sneak in with me." My cousin worked concessions in the local Cineworld, and she said she'd prop the fire exit open on Friday afternoon. And so, at the agreed time, I scurried across the front row of a semi-bustling auditorium, dressed in black and laying on the carpet directly under the screen. What followed was the defining movie experience of my life, 81 minutes that shaped me into the horror obsessive I am today.

Never before had I felt such a part of what I was watching, ripped from the silver screen and thrown into the terrifying woods of Burkittsville.

Mitch Harrod, aged eight (and one third), had survived *The Blair Witch Project*.

# Chapter Six

## The Haxan Five

It was going to take a team of determined, quick-thinking and highly original filmmakers to bring their idea to the big screen. The Haxan Five was born.

The name of the company is taken from the Swedish/Danish silent film – the word itself meaning "Witch". *Haxan: Witchcraft Through the Ages* (Benjamin Christensen, 1922) was a very unusual film for its time and is still a rather peculiar experience nowadays. The film was made in a documentary style as a study of superstition and the hysteria behind demons and witchcraft. The film successfully blends documentary-style narrative with dramatized sequences, creating an uneasy feeling of reality. The film was one of many that had been rented and watched while the team was looking for documentaries about witchcraft and the name seemed to stand out. It was Gregg who mentioned that it might be a good name for the production company that the group was forming.

The Haxan Five consisted of the aforementioned Eduardo Sanchez, Daniel Myrick and Gregg Hale, along with Robin Cowie (producer) and Michael Monello (co-producer).

### Gregg Hale

Gregg was in a year below Ed and Dan at film school and had admired the lighting work Dan had done for a number of productions. Gregg and Dan became friends after they worked together on Gregg's final film. After school Gregg moved to Los Angeles but the two stayed in touch. Gregg found work as a set dresser for a TV show, but while watching *Twelve Monkeys* (Terry Gilliam, 1995) he realised that he wanted to have an effect on people and couldn't do that unless he was making a movie. Gregg soon moved back to Florida and began working with Dan.

Once he was told the idea for the film, Gregg immediately became involved as a part of the team. A small office was set up and Gregg began to pitch the film to others. He found himself telling the story as if it was real and people were enthralled by it. The response was overwhelmingly positive and this, coupled with Ed and Dan's willingness to bring Gregg on board as a full partner, bolstered his energy and commitment to the project.

Gregg soon took on the role of the instigator. He would be there to push the production forward, initially because he had some money to pay for the travel and auditions. Gregg treated the film as a reality and knew wholeheartedly that it simply *had* to be made. As things moved forward, Gregg became more involved in the creative aspect of the film, in terms of what the characters were going to do, what they would encounter and how this would be conveyed by the filmmakers.

Gregg had previously spent time in the army and as part of his survival school training he found himself on a week-long "escape and evasion". Gregg was left in the woods with a small team and was forced to move from point-to-point at night, with no food or water. As you would imagine, things soon became unpleasant.

All of this was conducted in the context of a realistic survival scenario. Upon completion, the team were ambushed and taken away for a simulated interrogation in a very realistic wartime prison "set". After six days of no food, no sleep and being messed with, Gregg got a taste of *intense fear*. In a conversation with Ed and Dan the idea came up to put the actors through a similar scenario to the one that Gregg had encountered in survival school. The filmmakers would treat the actors this way for several days and by the time they would get to the end of it, they would be so completely freaked out, they would no longer be acting, just channeling the emotions that were really there. The only way that they could make the film look real was to create this situation and just let the actors go out and film it.

## Robin Cowie

Rob was also a student at UCF and met the rest of the group there. His first meeting was with Dan, who worked as director of photography on a music video that Rob was making. Rob then met and helped Gregg on a project before graduating and starting his own business making corporate and commercial videos.

At the same time that Gregg had moved back from Los Angeles, Rob decided that he needed to change directions and get more involved with cinematic work. The two crossed paths and Gregg at this time was pitching the idea of the film as if it was real. Rob was completely hooked and believed that the students were missing and there were tapes that had been uncovered showing their last days. Gregg fully explained what they were doing and recruited Rob to join the team.

Rob came on board at the perfect time. After getting the concept to a certain point Ed, Dan and Gregg had become frustrated trying to raise money for the film. The primary reason for Rob's involvement was to raise money for the project and to form a structure for the raising of that money. Rob got to work writing up the business plan and hiring the business attorney and then set out approaching people to invest in the film. Luckily Rob was able to invest some of his own money and also to bring in some money from friends and friends of friends who were interested in what the team was producing.

Rob started out as the financial guy and a problem solver and then joined in with the brainstorming. All aspects of the film were discussed to death, ideas thrown at the wall to see what stuck. As the film progressed, Rob found his responsibilities as a producer became more traditional with jobs including organising insurance, making sure bills were paid and deliverables allotted.

During the actual shoot of the film Rob was not on location, instead he was working to keep things running smoothly. A couple of days before the shoot there were permit issues with the park board who were managing the forest where the production was set to take place, as no one is allowed in the park overnight. Luckily Rob happened to know somebody who knew somebody on the board and was able to rectify this potentially disastrous situation.

## Michael Monello

The fifth member of the team was a friend of Ed and Dan at the UCF Film School. The three of them actually joined in the inaugural year of a new program designed for sixty students – fortunately for them there were only thirty students with access to the full resources of the school.

Ed, Dan and Mike worked on each other's films during the first year and then Rob and Gregg arrived the following year. Much later, when Ed told Mike the story of the *Blair Witch*, he thought it was incredible. The idea that they wanted to make something in the vein of creepy old documentaries and to able to turn regular filmmaking problems such as bad camera, sound and lighting into assets, appealed to him.

Mike didn't join the project as early as the others but he was there to help with the investor tapes and to create some mock news stories. Mike joined the filmmakers after Phase One had been shot. He was instrumental in helping out with connections as he worked on the Florida Film Festival and eventually hooked Dan up with John Pierson, an independent filmmaker with his own company, Grainy Pictures. John also had a television series called *Split Screen* which was one of the first shows to air a segment on the mythology of the *Blair Witch* and the missing students. This investor trailer was the first ever public exposure to the film and aired on August 15th 1997.

Gradually Mike became more and more involved; using the extensive publicity experience he had gained from working at the film festival to create a formidable marketing strategy for the project. It was at this point that Mike was brought into the team officially. Mike had specific contacts that were invaluable to the promotion of the film. His basic knowledge of the distributors, the kind of films they put out and how that worked really helped the project. Mike trusted his contacts enough that there was no risk of leaking any vital information regarding the reality of the project. This led to the first flurry of stories appearing in press, generating the buzz that was so necessary to the eventual success of the film. Mike was also fully on board when it came time to handle the film festival side of things, choosing, submitting and then dealing with the festivals, including Sundance.

## The Crew

A small, but dedicated and vital crew joined the Haxan Five to cover all areas of the production. Some members of this crew included Ben Rock, who came up with the team from Orlando and worked on the film as production designer. Ben coordinated with Ricardo Moreno, a childhood friend of Ed's who had lived in Maryland for many years. Rick was working at the time but his locality meant that he was in the perfect position to help the crew. It fell upon Ben to do all of the detail work: to dress the house, procure the props and create the now iconic stickman figures. Rick later ended up as the art director for the film.

At the time, Ben lived close to Gregg and the two would regularly catch up and talk about various projects. Ben had been working on effects for low budget monster movies and had been telling Gregg about his latest designs when Gregg launched into the story of the *Blair Witch*. He completely hooked Ben, who believed it all to be true. After eventually learning that the story was made up, Ben joined the crew and began work on fleshing out the legend and mythology – a perfect fit due to Ben's passion for folklore and the supernatural.

Neal Fredericks came in from Los Angeles to work as cinematographer on the film. Neal owned a CP-16 (a 16mm film camera manufactured by the Cinema Products Corporation of Hollywood California), which was used as the "A" camera on the production. Neal acted as a camera technician and taught basic cinematography and camera techniques to Joshua Leonard, who was to portray a cameraman in the film.

Antonio Cora, who is Ed's cousin, was bought in to help out with sound. Tony helped to get Mike Williams, who was playing the soundman in the film, familiar with sound recording and the equipment. Tony also recorded some of the creepy sounds and music for the film – most importantly the absolutely terrifying end credits track 'The Cellar'.

Lonnie Glerum became head P.A. (production assistant) for the film and did everything from driving to helping with the art department and assisting with on-set logistics. This was an all-important job that ensured all the little details were covered and taken care of. Lonnie was a friend of Ed and Rick's from high school and was Ed's roommate at UCF. Lonnie helped out on (and even starred in) some of Ed's first films in film school.

Matt Compton had moved to Los Angeles by the time the film shoot in Maryland began, but back in 1996 he was involved with production meetings with Ed and Dan and he also went out to scout locations before everyone arrived. Matt is responsible for finding the ever-so creepy building that was to be used in the final scenes of the film where Heather and Mike come across Rustin Parr's house.

This group of intrepid filmmakers packed up their gear ready for their trip to Maryland. Phase One of *The Blair Witch Project* was about to begin.

## The Blair Witch Experience

## Sean Plummer

*Sean Plummer is a Toronto-based but suburban-raised freelance writer, part-time Goth, and horror fan. He was editor at Canadian pop culture magazine* Access *from 1996 to 2010 and is a long-time contributor to* Rue Morgue Magazine. *His work has also appeared in* Details, The Toronto Star *and on* CBC Radio.

Word started leaking out about this mysterious horror movie, *The Blair Witch Project*, after its January premiere at the Sundance Film Festival. In those nascent online days, the website *blairwitch.com* suggested that the film was composed of real found footage. That sounded like bullshit, but as the editor of a Toronto-based pop culture magazine, I duly followed up with the film's local distributor, and requested a screening and interview with one of its directors.

Probably around May 1999, in order to make my long lead time, I was invited to a private screening of the film. With me in that small room were just a few theatre owners and two colleagues from the horror magazine *Rue Morgue*. Our expectations were low since there was little definitive information available about the film, just rumours.

We all left that room shaken and disturbed. Not knowing what to expect, I was broadsided by the film's apparent reality. It looked real. More importantly, it felt real.

Shortly thereafter I interviewed Eduardo Sanchez by phone, the reality was restored and my article became part of the avalanche of hype that helped make *The Blair Witch Project* a global phenomenon. Re-watching the film, I've never been so scared again as I was initially, of course, but I thank it for making me feel real fear that one time.

# Chapter Seven

## The legend of Elly Kedward

*The Blair Witch Project* hinged on a very incredible and believable mythology. Not just for the audiences but for the characters in the film. Creating realism was vital at this point and no stone could be left unturned. If this was going to work it was going to have to be completely watertight and indisputable for everyone outside of the production team.

Hours and hours of long brainstorming sessions led to the backstory of Elly Kedward and the town of Blair being born.

I have a great love of tales, myths and legends, so the creation of the *Blair Witch* world is one of the key elements for me. It was an aspect of storytelling that I had never seen before. I was learning so much before even seeing the film – things that were essential to shaping my overall impression of the film. I would read and re-read the history from the website, imagining how all of this stuff happened and trying to piece the mystery together.

What follows is the full timeline of major events in the history of the *Blair Witch* as taken from the original website. This timeline is the backbone of the story. Gregg, Ed and Dan came up with the outline for the backstory and gave it to Ben, who then proceeded to fill in the details – all of the names, dates and locations. Ed then took the timeline and added it to the website to give readers a mythology they could discover for themselves.

It is incredible to read this document, even now. It oozes with creativity and shows a real passion for the project, but more than that it highlights how the filmmakers knew exactly the lengths they would have to go to in order to make this film work, both as a terrifying piece of cinema and a completely believable story. It is the creation of the following mythology that really made *The Blair Witch Project* feel real, terrifying and even unsafe.

## The History of the Blair Witch:

The Township of Blair was located in North Central Maryland, two hours from Washington, D.C.

*February 1785*
Several children accuse Elly Kedward of luring them into her home to draw blood from them. Kedward is found guilty of witchcraft, banished from the village during a particularly harsh winter and presumed dead.

*November 1786*
By midwinter all of Kedward's accusers along with half of the town's children vanish. Fearing a curse, the townspeople flee Blair and vow never to utter Elly Kedward's name again.

*November 1809*
*The Blair Witch Cult* is published. This rare book, commonly considered fiction, tells of an entire town cursed by an outcast witch.

*1824*
Burkittsville is founded on the Blair site.

*August 1825*
Eleven witnesses testify to seeing a pale woman's hand reach up and pull ten-year-old Eileen Treacle into Tappy East Creek. Her body is never recovered, and for thirteen days after the drowning the creek is clogged with oily bundles of sticks.

*March 1886*
Eight-year-old Robin Weaver is reported missing and search parties are dispatched. Although Weaver returns, one of the search parties does not. Their bodies are found weeks later at Coffin Rock tied together at the arms and legs and completely disembowelled.

*November 1940 - May 1941*
Starting with Emily Hollands, a total of seven children are abducted from the area surrounding Burkittsville, Maryland.

*May 25th 1941*
An old hermit named Rustin Parr walks into a local market and tells the people there that he is "finally finished." After Police hike for four hours to his secluded house in the woods, they find the bodies of seven missing children in the cellar. Each child has been ritualistically murdered and disemboweled. Parr admits to everything in detail, telling authorities that he did it for "an old woman ghost" who occupied the woods near his house. He is quickly convicted and hanged.

*October 20th 1994*
Montgomery College students Heather Donahue, Joshua Leonard, and Michael Williams arrive in Burkittsville to interview locals about the legend of the Blair Witch for a class project. Heather interviews Mary Brown, an old and quite insane woman who has lived in the area all her life. Mary claims to have seen the Blair Witch one day near Tappy Creek in the form of a hairy, half-human, half-animal beast.

October 21st 1994
In the early morning Heather interviews two fishermen who tell the filmmakers that Coffin Rock is less than twenty minutes from town and easily accessible by an old logging trail. The filmmakers hike into Black Hills Forest shortly thereafter and are never seen again.

October 25th 1994
The first APB is issued. Josh's car is found later in the day parked on Black Rock Road.

*October 26th 1994*
The Maryland State Police launch their search of the Black Hills area, an operation that lasts ten days and includes up to one hundred men aided by dogs, helicopters, and even a flyover by a Department of Defense Satellite.

*November 5th 1994*
The search is called off after 33,000 man hours fail to find a trace of the filmmakers or any of their gear. Heather's mother, Angie Donahue, begins an exhaustive personal search for her daughter and her two companions.

*June 19th 1995*
The case is declared inactive and unsolved.

*October 16th 1995*
Students from the University of Maryland's Anthropology Department discover a duffel bag containing film cans, DAT tapes, video-cassettes, a Hi-8 video camera, Heather's journal and a CP-16 film camera buried under the foundation of a 100 year-old cabin. When the evidence is examined, Burkittsville Sheriff Ron Cravens announced that the 11 rolls of black and white film and 10 HI8 video tapes are indeed the property of Heather Donahue and her crew.

*December 15th 1995*
After an initial study of the bag's contents, select pieces of film footage are shown to the families. According to Angie Donahue, there are several unusual events but nothing conclusive. The families question the thoroughness of the analysis and demanded another look.

*February 19th 1996*
The families are shown a second group of clips that local law enforcement officials consider to be faked. Outraged, Mrs. Donahue goes public with her criticism and Sheriff Cravens restricts all access to the evidence; a restriction that two lawsuits fail to lift.

*March 1st 1996*
The Sheriff's department announces that the evidence is inconclusive and the case is once again declared inactive and unsolved. The footage is to be released to the families when the legal limit of its classification runs out, on October 16, 1997.

*October 16th 1997*
The found footage of their children's last days is turned over to the families of Heather Donahue, Joshua Leonard, and Michael Williams. Angie Donahue contracts Haxan Films to examine the footage and piece together the events of October 20–28, 1994.

## The Blair Witch Experience

## Joe Lynch

*Joe Lynch is a director, or at least he keeps telling people that. Born in Long Island and dealing with life in L.A., Lynch's previous films include such seminal cinematic classics as* Wrong Turn 2: Dead End *(2007),* Knights of Badassdom *(2013),* Chillerama *(2011),* Everly *(2014), starring Salma Hayek and* Mayhem *(2017), starring Steven Yeun. @TheJoeLynch*

I saw *The Blair Witch Project* at Sundance when it played there before the hoopla began. People were talking in hushed tones that the festival had accepted its first "snuff film". Immediately I was interested.

I was in Park City with Troma promoting *Terror Firmer* with president Lloyd Kaufman and writer Patrick Cassidy and one of my duties was to represent Troma as the Toxic Avenger. Lloyd would make me dress up in that vile costume for all the screenings I'd go to, including the premiere of Antonia Bird's *Ravenous* at Sundance that year. So here I am, in this costume that has never been washed, with a mask that smells like my vomit from the day before (another story for another day), sitting in *Ravenous* next to Roger Ebert, and it isn't going well. Everyone walked out of the movie a little bummed, but as the crowd was gathering in the lobby, another movie got out. Taking the Toxie mask off for air, I noticed that the audience for the other theatre looked as if they had seen a ghost.

On the bus back up the hill I approached one of them and after the shock of a half-dressed mutant superhero from New Jersey wore off, the woman said that yes, they had just witnessed a "snuff film". Needless to say, I was up at 4am the following day to get standby tickets for the next show.

We had heard there were no post-screening Q&As, which only added to the myth of the footage shown. However, when I saw it (and was blown away) they did bring the filmmakers out which finally made it clear that this was all designed and not real. But up until that point, I honestly thought I was watching true horror, dread and death onscreen.

Knowing Troma could never acquire the rights to *The Blair Witch Project* but noticing the similarities to another movie, I immediately went back to New York and told Lloyd to get the rights to *Cannibal Holocaust* (Ruggero Deodato, 1980) and to release it when *The Blair Witch Project* would hit. At the time there weren't a lot of fake documentaries other than David Holtzman's *Diary* (Jim McBride, 1967) or *Man Bites Dog* (Rémy Belvaux, André Bonzel & Benoît Poelvoorde, 1992).

Funnily enough, when we did get back, our editor Gabe happened on a VHS copy of *The Blair Witch Project*, which we passed around like the tape from *Ringu* (Hideo Nakata, 1998), not telling anyone anything – hearing their reactions was amazing. It was fascinating being an "early adopter", before the hype machine started, to really see how people reacted watching what they thought was real, back before internet beheadings and a multitude of found footage films dulled the effect.

Later I heard of *Curse of the Blair Witch*, but since I was already very aware of the film's origins and the mythology that the team at Haxan Films and Artisan (the distributor) was developing, it had less of an impact on me. I of course watched the Sci-Fi Channel special but, honestly, in the school of "less is more" I didn't need all the backstory, the explaining.

To me, what made the first film special was the lack of knowledge of the witch. That only made me delve into the narrative more on my own, trying to figure things out, and invested me in the initial story. The more they keep trying to uncover the truth, the more the witch gets demystified, it takes the piss out of the scares.

*The Blair Witch Project* deeply affected me on many levels. As I was watching it for the first time, thinking it was very real and forgetting any idea that it could be staged, that true feeling of horror unfolded; the confusion and chaos of what lies in the shadows of the night. This film tapped into so many base fears that we all have, even today, and offered no apologies at the end, which I admired. They could have presented us with a reveal, that it was all fake, but that they didn't only added to the impact. Plus, how inspiring that these indie filmmakers with little to no money came up with a concept that fit the budget parameters and even enhanced it, by essentially baking-in the characters as a crew, making the actors do the heavy lifting while the Haxan team ran around in the dark REALLY trying to scare the cast – that's some method shit right there. And their little indie ended up opening over the summer with the quote "Scarier Than *The Exorcist*", which is the dream quote for any genre filmmaker. These guys and girls did it using their own rules and changed the genre and the process of filmmaking itself, showing that anyone with a few cameras and friends could make a movie as long as you had the right story. It was very exciting.

One thing that I loved was the "Missing" posters they created to help market the movie. About three to four months before the film came out, while I was passing the VHS tape around like a giddy sadist to unassuming audiences, the posters started popping up all over NYC. Nothing about the movie or the studio, no hint that this was "fake news" so to speak; just a very plan, stark flyer with the "filmmakers" faces on it and that was it. You see that enough times plastered around New York City and you're gonna take notice. To see how people were already concerned for these three not even knowing they were characters in a movie coming out soon was really clever and invested the audience immediately. The whole campaign they did for the original was a masterclass in marketing.

# Chapter Eight

## The Woods Movie

Production of the film began with an initial title of *The Woods Movie*. There were several other titles for the film at the time, including *The Black Hills Project* and *The Blair Witch Tapes*. While brainstorming, Ed came up with the idea of the three missing college kids coming from Montgomery College – the school he originally went to before UCF. It had been earlier in the process when Dan and Ed were emailing the treatment back and forth that Ed decided they needed a title. The name Blair came into his head and he liked it (Ed's sister Adriana had gone to Blair High School). Ed figured they would come up with a better name for the film later on, but the name stuck. The film was to be known as *The Blair Witch Project*.

With their new title in place the next step was to find three individuals who were willing and able to take on the almost insane task of portraying the three leads in the film. In the summer of 1996 the audition process began. Over the course of a year and almost a thousand auditions, the perfect leads were found. Joshua Leonard was picked first and joined the process, eventually helping to find Heather Donahue and Michael Williams.

The next job was to secure the rest of the money needed for the initial proposed $25,000 budget. The idea was to produce a footage reel to show around to potential investors. They produced an eight minute short entitled *The Blair Witch Project: The Story of the Black Hills Disappearances*. This very creepy and enthralling video contained a brief history of witchcraft and a history of the Blair Witch of Maryland, before detailing how three student filmmakers had gone missing while making a documentary about the witch and how police had released the footage to Haxan Films to piece together.

Many investors completely believed in what they saw, which gave the Haxan team both their budget and the realisation that what they were doing already had gained a level of credibility from some fairly important people. The intended budget for the film was completed with money from airing their investor reel on *Split Screen*. They were paid for this segment, and also for a second segment that would be edited together from the real footage they were about to shoot.

In October 1997 the team assembled in Maryland to shoot the first part of the film. Most of the month was spent out in the woods planning and preparing everything for the locations that the actors would be using. In the first couple of weeks of October, much fun was to be had as the gang spent a night at the derelict house in the woods doing camera and lighting tests while Gregg was made up to look like a ghost and ran around in the woods. Excursions (and inevitable heated discussions) to purchase tents, army camouflage and other necessities for the shoot also took place at this time along with the drama of overspending on string for the art department. [4]

Stefanie and Carolyn DeCassan and Julia Fair also joined the team during trips out to the woods to build more stickmen and create sinister rock piles. Ben spent an incredible amount of time preparing the house for the final scenes and creating new and improved stickmen to hang in the woods, including the gigantic "Chewbacca" stickman which can be seen clearly in the film.

On 19th October the actors arrived and began their pre-production phase of becoming the film versions of themselves. During the next couple of days they stayed together at a hotel and went about filming various things, including an investigation of a local legend – Cry Baby Bridge. Heather had already begun to write the infamous journal that would become part of the legend later on during the "investigation into their disappearance".

Between October 23rd and October 30th history was written as Josh, Heather and Mike ventured further and further into Seneca Creek State Park (known as the Black Hills Forest for the film) just outside Gaithersburg, Maryland. The drama soon took over and much of what is seen on screen is a realistic portrayal of three kids in a stressful situation. They knew little of what would happen to them over the course of the week and had only been given brief details before leaving for the

---

4 "Damn Twine!"

woods. Heather even took a newly purchased hunting knife with her just in case sleeping in a tent with two guys became a little dangerous.

Heather, Mike and Josh weren't told if the Blair Witch and the mythology was true or not, creating a sense of unease as they set off into the woods. It also helped that during earlier scenes some of the townsfolk they had interviewed were secretly planted by the directors[5]. This "fictional reality" helped to push the actors into a completely frantic and emotional state which left them with a genuine concern for their own safety. This led to some highly charged and very realistic scenes – footage that the film just couldn't have done without.

Gregg introduced the idea of GPS. The production used this new technology and the three actors were issued with the military-grade global positioning system to guide them to the designated filming locations. They would come across a waypoint where three small 35mm film tubes had been left for them. Each tube was marked with the initials H, M or J and gave the individuals a unique set of directing notes. This enabled Ed and Dan to direct from afar and to keep the actors in the scenario. It also helped to create a sense of confusion and realism as they never really knew too much about what would happen ahead of time. The team would watch as much of the footage as possible (which wasn't much, due to the crazy schedule). Ed would type up notes and get input from Dan. Gregg would supply the logistical information that would be added to the notes. The notes were then put in the tubes and left out in the wilderness to keep the actors on track for the day ahead. These notes would give basic scene directions and brief location details for the day. Crew members worked in teams and took turns hiding out in the woods following the actors' moves while dressed in camouflage gear. They would wait for nightfall before building rock formations outside their tents, hanging the stickman figures from the trees and, worst of all, playing tapes of the sounds of crying children. They all took turns running around the woods making noises, terrifying their actors in the middle of the night.

---

5 These even included Ed's own sister, Sandra, in the scene at Silver Rail Diner.

The intense ordeal led to many unscripted outbursts and real dramatic situations, each day pushing the three actors to their very limits and capturing the moments on film. However, a very safety-conscious production team was never far behind, just in case of emergency.

One such emergency arose on day four of principle photography. The rain had slowed the production team down and actually pushed the actors to move faster. This meant that the actors arrived at their location for the day before it had been set up. The actors, worried that something was seriously wrong, attempted a radio check with basecamp but to no avail. It was time to use the safe word, the term that would only be used if the actors were in desperate need of breaking the scenario – "BULLDOZER!" The actors freaked out and made their way in the rain to a nearby house (where they were treated to warm towels and hot drinks) and used the telephone to call the production team. The actors were taken to a motel for the night to recover while their tents and equipment were taken to dry off also. The day's filming had to be reset in the morning.

The process continued until the final day of principal photography on Saturday 1st November 1997. This was to be a night of reshoots as the previous night had given the production continuous trouble with battery power. This was also the night that would deliver some of the most intense and unsettling scenes of realism as Heather and Mike reached the end of their journey in the basement of the old Parr house.

There was a huge sense of relief as production wrapped that night.

The remaining few months of 1997 were spent trying to reclaim some sense of normality and preparing for the next steps, while still trying to watch and log over twenty hours of footage that had been captured over the eight full days of shooting. For many this would be an unbearable chore, but for this fan it was an honour to sit down over several days, years later, and watch all of the raw footage that had been shot in the woods – along with the twenty something hours of behind the scenes footage that detailed the production from early meetings to victory at Sundance.[6]

---

6 Later edited into the feature documentary, *The Woods Movie* (Russ Gomm, 2015)

Ed and Dan made VHS copies of all of the footage and then began making notes on what they would be able to use for the film. They began to cut the footage down to a shorter length but it was still eight hours of great footage that could be used.

Finding themselves short of money one of the two Hi-8 cameras used in the film was promptly returned to Circuit City under the thirty-day money-back guarantee. The team's vision was only half realised, so in order to start work on Phase Two a further $35,000 was raised.

The next step in the production was to last almost another year. Phase Two included editing the footage from the woods and shooting all of the mythology that had been created, including interviews and old documentary footage. Ed had previously worked as a web designer and knew enough to develop a very interesting aspect of the project and what would become the most impressive marketing scheme ever seen for a film up to that point. The official website went live in May 1998 and gained instant attention – especially from the fans that had already been accumulated from the *Split Screen* online discussion boards. Those were the first people to visit the website and they visited often. The website offered minimal information but began to sow the seeds of what was coming soon.

## The Blair Witch Experience

## Matt Blazi

*Matt Blazi has been a fan of* The Blair Witch Project *since 1999. Since 2013 he has organised the Official Blair Witch Facebook group and has led "The Blair Witch Experience", an annual tour and camping trip covering all of the locations that were used in the film.*

I was a horror movie fan from a very early age, starting with zombies and branching out to the other horror icons. As I grew up I discovered more and decided I needed to see as many horror films as I could get my hands on.

At the age of 18, I stumbled upon a trailer for *The Blair Witch Project*.

I remember being completely enthralled by it. It wasn't something I had seen before. There was almost nothing on screen to tell me about the film, but the music was absolutely chilling. The trailer made me want to know more. I was getting ready to graduate high school and I remember I must have been talking about it a lot because my dad asked me about it. I told him it wasn't something I knew much about, but I had to see it.

I spent the summer of 1999 reading everything I could find about the film. As the time drew nearer I became more and more swept up by the hype. I never thought the film was real but it stood out because it wasn't promoted like any other film. There was nothing about it outside of people talking. The directors and actors weren't really on talk shows or anything that would give me insight into the film. I remember seeing *Curse of the Blair Witch* before the film. It was the perfect piece of promotional material to get me ready.

The weeks between seeing *Curse of the Blair Witch* and the film itself seemed to be the longest time for a kid waiting to see a movie.

The theatre I saw the movie in on opening day was sold out. I sat near the front with my girlfriend at the time. I was ready for the film, but wasn't ready for what I saw. When the film ended and the music hit I was in shock. Not a bad shock, but an "I can't believe I just saw that" kind of shock. I ended up seeing it again a few days later.

Three weeks later I went off to college and I was there just twenty-four hours before I ventured to the tattoo parlour to have the stickman tattooed on my shoulder. I saw the film again in the theatre a few weeks later. I decorated my dorm room in

*Blair Witch* posters and memorabilia. A friend of mine even started calling me "Blair Witch" due to this obsession.

The more I talked about it, the more people would ask me about it and tell me they thought it was real and wanted to know more. I found every website made for the film and devoured all the information I could find. I downloaded wallpapers, icons, desktop themes, everything. I listened to the soundtrack endlessly and even ended up with a VHS screener of the film from a friend who knew someone at a local theatre.

After the hype eventually died down, *The Blair Witch Project* sort of became a background phenomenon to me. I didn't talk about it but from time to time people would recognize my tattoo. In 2000 I visited the house (while it was standing). In 2012 a friend of mine made a video exploring all the locations of the film. To me it was a crowning achievement of fandom for the film. After seeing his video I decided I needed to see the rest of the locations for myself.

In 2013 I mapped out where the locations were and Ed Sanchez helped me to fill in the gaps. I visited a few times, took many pictures and shared them online. The more I shared, the more people came out of the woodwork, showing love for the film. A friend suggested we tour and camp out nearby for a weekend that fall and I agreed. I started talking to friends about the trip and building momentum – even Ed suggested he may join us.

I made a Facebook event and shared it, figuring nobody would come, but I ended up having five people join me on the first trip. It was small and intimate, but a lot of fun. Ed came out and showed us where they filmed the rock cemetery scene and where the stickmen were hung – two locations that were holy grails for me. After the weekend I started a Facebook group for *Blair Witch* as there wasn't a real online presence for it. Since 2014 the group has grown to include cast and crew of both the original *The Blair Witch Project* and now the new film. The community is that celebrates and keeps the spirit of the film alive. When I started it, I just wanted it to be a small gathering of fans and it has grown to a level I never anticipated.

The biggest thing I have personally taken away from *The Blair Witch Project* is the connections I've made because of it. That doesn't just stop at connecting with the cast and crew of the film but connecting fans to other fans. Seeing groups of friends come together because of my admiration for a film is more fulfilling than anything I do for myself. Friends of mine have now become friends with each other because of me. "The Blair Witch Experience" each year brings more fans closer to their favourite film, as well as an opportunity to meet up with other likeminded individuals.

These connections are more important that talking with a cast or crew member, they forge friendships for life. That is what *The Blair Witch Project* means to me.

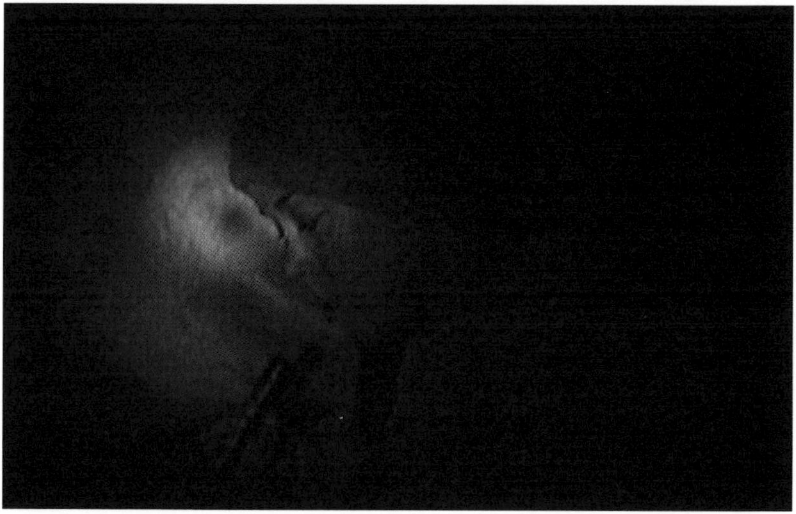

# Chapter Nine

## Phase two

When a little eight-minute documentary on the film aired in April 1998 on the John Pierson show *Split Screen*, viewers were sent into frenzy. Editing of the feature film continued and the first cut was completed with a running time of two and a half hours. They knew it was at least an hour too long, but needed feedback on what they were doing. This cut was screened at the Enzian Theater on 27th June 1998 to get initial reactions – was the story convincing enough? Did the characters come across as genuine? How much backstory was necessary?

It transpired that most were utterly terrified by what they saw.

Among the audience members was Kevin Foxe, an independent filmmaker based in Los Angeles. He was blown away and put Haxan Films on the path to entering the film into the Sundance Film Festival. Kevin came on board during post-production and became an executive producer, pushing the film even further than the team could have ever imagined.

*The Blair Witch Project* was originally envisaged to have a documentary portion included. These scenes would have included information about the *Blair Witch* legend and mythology and also would be an examination of the footage that had been left by the students. This was the Phase Two footage. After this first test screening the reaction was great – the film was scary and everyone was intrigued, buy they wanted more information about the legend. The video that the students shot seemed to be so strong and stand up on its own, but there was room for some mythology.

Phase Two went into production and Ed and Dan began to use these new scenes in conjunction with the original video footage. Some of the new material they filmed included "old" 16mm footage of Rustin Parr in jail, being questioned about his crimes, and a fake vintage occult show named Mystic Occurrences which appeared to be from 1971 and showed Lucan Johnson, a Wiccan, explaining witchcraft and recounting some of the legend of the *Blair Witch*. The filmmakers were still going to every length to make the reality of *The Blair Witch Project* indisputable.

Editing continued and different versions of the film were worked on simultaneously to ascertain what would play best with audiences. Dan worked on a version of the film where the Phase Two scenes were interspersed with the footage of the students. This subsequently played out like a documentary. Conversely, Ed's version concentrated all of the new scenes at the beginning of the film before showing any of the "found footage".

Eventually it became obvious that the Phase Two footage was draining the tension from the video scenes that the students had shot. In the end, Phase Two became a five minute introduction at the start of the film, which the two directors agreed on. They finalised the film and sent it off to Kevin in Los Angeles, who maintained that the film was stronger in its original incarnation, without any of the Phase Two footage. This latest cut robbed the film of its intensity.

Phase Two did not work.

A 100-minute version of the film was then screened to another test audience at the University of Central Florida, where the filmmakers had originally attended school. It went well and there was much feedback gained from the screening. In October, after a great deal of discussion and further editing, the film was finally cut down to 87 minutes and deemed good enough for a real world audience. It was entered into the Sundance Film Festival.

It would soon become clear just how good it was.

News was received that *The Blair Witch Project* had been accepted into the Festival.

In January 1999 the team at Haxan Films travelled (some in shorts) from sunny Florida to the cold, snowy paradise known as Park City, Utah, for Sundance.

Saturday January 23rd 1999 would be the night that changed everything. The screening took place in the midnight slot and had attracted so much attention that it sold out fast. Nearly two hundred people had to be turned away. The screening went better than anyone could have ever expected and it led to Gregg and Rob spending the rest of the night with executives from Artisan Entertainment. Ed and Dan went back to their hotels to sleep. Little did they know that at 3am Gregg would call to say that Artisan Entertainment wanted the buy the film. Every half hour Gregg would update them on the progress until one final call at 6am was made simply to inform them that they had sold the movie to Artisan Entertainment for $1.1 million.

Executives at Artisan were unsure of the ending of the film and agreed to finance reshoots. Four alternate endings and some more Phase Two mythology footage was shot with this budget. Ben Rock, Rick Moreno and other crew-members re-joined the team and Rob and Michael (who had not been on location for the original shoot) got to visit the Parr house for the first time. This was a much more pleasant shoot – people were getting paid – and fun was had. Nevertheless, Ed and Dan fought for their ending, despite a warning from Artisan that they would lose money if they did. However, in the end they were vindicated. The alternate endings didn't work and, ultimately, it was decided to stick with the original finale.

The film went back to the editing room briefly with a few small changes here and there. The sound mix on the film was dramatically improved and a couple of new scenes were added to help audiences understand the sinister ending of the film. A new 82-minute version of the film was completed in time for the trip to the Cannes Film Festival where the film played successfully and gained the Prix De Jeunesse Award.

After returning from Cannes work commenced on the forty-five minute documentary *Curse of the Blair Witch*. Ed and Dan directed the TV special and Ben was asked to come on board once again to help write the project. It was edited by Michael Monello. This documentary contained a lot of the Phase Two footage that had been shot and detailed the entire history of the Blair Witch and the mystery of the missing college students. All of the hard work in creating a full and believable mythology was to pay off. The documentary was designed to be the perfect preamble to the full feature, containing all the information viewers would need to fully appreciate the film. It spread the fear and viewers believed what they had seen. The hysteria that was generated was unprecedented. The documentary premiered nationwide in America on July 11th, just a few days before the film itself was to be screened to the public, and led to a major uplift of traffic to the website.

The premiere was in New York City on July 14th 1999. There was a packed house. The screening was so busy that the guys had trouble getting into their own film. The cinema displayed an exhibition of Blair Witch artefacts to further fool the viewers into believing the legend that had been created for them. It worked and two days later the film opened on twenty seven screens across America. At the beginning of each day most performances were fast becoming sold out. Over the opening weekend the film made an incredible $1.5 million dollars and was already a financial success. The following week the film opened on over a thousand more screens and nearly $30 million had soon been made at the box office. During its nine-week run at cinemas across America, the film earned an incredible $140 million. Another $100 million was added to that total when the film was taken overseas.

Upon release the film was completely unstoppable. For its many viewers *The Blair Witch Project* was a nausea-inducing hour and a half of pure terror as we watched the last days of Heather, Mike and Josh unfold before us. The very idea that the footage was real was both thought-provoking and horrifying. However the creation of a feature film using this found footage technique was just a very small piece of the puzzle that was the mystery of the Blair Witch.

## The Blair Witch Experience

## Dave Stern

*D.A. Stern is a multi-hyphenate: a successful author-publisher-game concocter.* The New York Times *bestsellers* Crosley, Lara Croft, Shadows in the Asylum *and a little slice of popular culture known as* Star Trek *are among his creative credentials. Mr. Stern is well plugged-into the many platforms the Blair Witch resides in. He and his family live in a creepy old house on a hill in Western Massachusetts. How creepy? His lawn Will Not Stop Growing!*

Dan Slater, who I had become friendly with when we were both editors at Pocket Books in New York, was working for NAL (New American Library Publishing), and had gotten wind of the entire *Blair Witch* phenomenon via Sundance.

Dan bought the rights to do books based on the movie for NAL, then called me up and told me all about it. He asked me to get involved as a writer for a book entitled *The Blair Witch Project: A Dossier*. I came to New York with Dan and sat down at a big conference table with everyone from Haxan Films. They showed me a ton of mythology materials they had already created and we discussed how to best present that material in a book context.

I think (and this is so long ago now I can't claim to be one hundred percent accurate in my recollections) that I came up with the idea of the detective agency searching for the truth. I had been working in an editorial capacity with Diane Ahlquist (who features as the psychic in the *Dossier*) on a separate project of her own and brought her into the mix as well. A lot of the photos in the book were actually photos of people at the publishing company, posing as characters from the novel.

Working on this particular project was the most exciting and involving experience I've ever had working on a tie-in property. This was in part because the guys from Haxan – Ed, Dan, Ben, Mike, Gregg Rob, et al – were not only open to my ideas, but they actively encouraged me to be as creative as possible. We were on such a tight deadline for the project that it was really a case of pulling together and just getting stuff done.

I remember thinking how cool it was that they were able to fit some of the backstory into the film. What I remember better than the movie, in fact, was standing in the middle of it, and seeing the entire phenomenon take off.

# Chapter Ten

## The curse of The Blair Witch

Soon *Blair Witch* was everywhere. Newspapers, magazines, television, radio. Marketing had turned to merchandise. Fans were eager for shirts, badges, key rings, hats, trading cards, comics, video games and anything else that had the infamous stickman on it, including that stupidly rare Japanese cuddly toy, 'The Missing Bear'. *Josh's Blair Witch Mix* was released and presented as the cassette tape found in Josh's car parked on Black Rock Road. The soundtrack CD became another part of the legend, further intensifying the myth. Probably the strangest collectible was the actual town sign from Burkittsville, which was stolen three times before being revamped as hundreds of believing fans descended upon the small town.

A very interesting piece of marketing was the aforementioned book *The Blair Witch Project: A Dossier* by D.A. Stern. The contents include police files, journals, letters and historical documents, as well as a disturbing account where the families of the missing students, with the help of private investigator Buck Buchanan (also seen in the documentary) and psychic Diane Ahlquist, try to uncover more about the events that took place in the woods. The book is both informative and extremely creepy.

There are many other unusual pieces of merchandise relating to the film. Some of my personal favourites include a CD by an unknown (and hard to track down) band called Sisyphus. Their album *Greetings from Burkittsville* has very little information on the CD except for the intriguing text: *Start (14:30) Camera Slate at Coffin Rock*. If you play the film and start the CD at fourteen and a half minutes in, you get a very unofficial – and very bizarre – soundtrack.

For PC gamers, there was a trilogy of *Blair Witch* games released between October and November 2000. They were very atmospheric and a lot of fun to play, delving somewhat into the history and mythology. And then there were both variant versions of the Todd McFarlane Blair Witch figure...

Upon the release of *The Blair Witch Project* in the UK in October of 1999 at least some of the impact of the film had already been lost. Remember, films often used to get an earlier release in America. Many people in the UK are probably still unaware of the effect the film had on American audiences who had less time to consider and question the publicity and marketing being used. The film had an absolutely huge marketing campaign in America, but by the time it reached UK soil it didn't need too much help along. News of reactions to the film overseas was enough to cause people to flock to cinemas en masse.

Unfortunately the UK audiences were divided upon seeing the film. This is understandable when you consider that so many vital ingredients were missing. *Curse of the Blair Witch* never aired in the UK (although I did once find a VHS copy to rent at Blockbuster Video) and without this, the audience didn't have any of the legend or background to prepare them for what they were watching.

I have always wondered what it would have been like to see the film cold, without any prior knowledge of the film. Would it have been as scary to me? Would it all make sense or would it just be running around in the woods with no real ending? Would I have enjoyed the film as much?

It had been such a long build-up in the four months between seeing the documentary and finally sitting down in a dark and crowded ABC Cinema on Halloween night to watch the film. I remember feeling equally worried and terrified watching the film. My mind was racing and my heart was pounding. I felt safe with the scenes that were set during the day, but once it got to night and the threat of the witch loomed closer I became a quivering mess. I was relieved when the film ended – partly because I could relax and partly because I had finally ticked the box of seeing this film. But something stayed with me for a long time afterwards. I still thought it was real. There was no doubt in my mind. I have a clear memory of the end credits rolling after the film, while that terrifying piece of music played. Unusually, I didn't read any of the credits – I was too much in shock. I remember when they finished and the lights in the cinema came up there was no sound. No one moved. An entire audience just sat there, not moving, not really knowing what to say or do. I've never seen anything like that.

I couldn't sleep that night. I wondered what had happened to the three students. I wondered if the witch was still out there. I convinced myself to stay out of the woods for a long time. I couldn't stop thinking about the film for weeks, months. It was all consuming.

Of course I bought the film on VHS (and then DVD and then Blu-Ray), but I was still so terrified that I didn't watch it again for a long time. I wanted to own it, but I never wanted to see it again. No other film has ever had such an effect on me.

The film was a huge success, taking $1.5 million on the opening weekend across twenty seven screens in America then going on to gross nearly $250 million worldwide – this was largely due to the incredible marketing campaign. Word of mouth and outstanding critical reviews made this the must-see film of 1999 and the *Blair Witch* a household name.

Granted, not everybody liked the film – but the negative reviews were outnumbered by the sheer amount of positivity.

Charles Mudede writes for Seattle free paper, *The Stranger* on July 15-21 1999:

*"Panic is exactly what the stunning, extremely unsettling new film* The Blair Witch Project *is all about – panic charged by fear of the unseen, of unreason; the monster lurking behind the trees, the spirits among the leaves, the dead under the stones, the souls in the river."*

When Roger Ebert's review appeared in the *Seattle Weekender* on July 16th 1999 the headline read:

"Witch Project *brilliantly uses imagination for its scares"*

...and continued to divulge more about his thoughts on the film in this four-star review:

*"At a time when digital techniques can show us almost anything,* The Blair Witch Project *is a reminder that what really scares us is the stuff we can't see"*

Susan Wloszczyna writes in *USA Today* on July 16th 1999:

*"This is low budget horror at its resourceful best, in the same nail-biting league as* Night of the Living Dead.*"*

She also wrote a short article for the cover of *USA Today* Life section on 14th July 1999:

*"The suspense becomes so unbearable that it's easy to overlook questions about whether anyone in such circumstances would continue filming. But then Heather, her startled eyes like those of a cornered rabbit, bares her soul in a shattering confessional, and you realize that* The Blair Witch Project *has you under its well-cast spell."*

In the UK, Matt Mueller wrote for *Total Film* in November 1999:

*"Too much hype can damage a movies health, but if you've managed to keep your distance, this hyper-realistic mockumentary will scare you witless without grossing you out. One of those rare films with the power to haunt long after the final frame."*

Years later, critics are still captivated by the film, with David Hughes writing in 2014 for *Empire Magazine*:

*"Whether your reaction to the film was, "That was some scary shit", or, "That was super-smart", depended largely on your own ability, or willingness, to suspend disbelief. Swept into the cinema on a wave of hype, or watching years later at home, you might even have greeted the film with a resounding "Meh". But as an exercise in making movies without money, inducing paranoia without production value, and conjuring scares without special effects,* The Blair Witch Project *is more than worthy of the Masterpiece mantle."*

# The Blair Witch Experience

## Alan Jones

*Alan Jones is an international film critic, broadcaster and bestselling author. The first film he covered on location was* Star Wars *(George Lucas, 1977), the latest* Ghost Stories *(Andy Nyman & Jeremy Dyson, 2017). His highly acclaimed books include:* Dario Argento: The Man, The Myth & The Magic, The Rough Guide to Horror Movies, Saturday Night Forever: The Story of Disco and The Act of Seeing, *the latter in collaboration with director Nicolas Winding Refn. He is a director of FrightFest, the UK's top fantasy festival, and is currently working on a TV project with Eli Roth.*

When all the hype started swirling around the Sundance Film Festival showing of directors Daniel Myrick and Eduardo Sanchez' *The Blair Witch Project* in January 1999, I must admit I was intrigued like everyone else. I'd heard it all before, of course, with other built-up genre movies touted with the likes of "a game-changer", "a phenomenon", "an unexpected masterpiece". But this one had a definite unique air about it mainly because of the wholly innovative internet marketing aspects. In retrospect did gullible students really believe it was authentic? If they did then I have a cursed videotape I want them to watch.

It took an inordinate amount of time to convince the UK distributor Pathé to actually show their canny acquisition to anyone. It was clear their press office just didn't get it, weren't sure what to do with it and were more frightened of fucking it up with a PR campaign so close to the once bitten unrepeatable "Is it fake, you decide" campaign than the movie itself. I remember all the key British critical fraternity packed into a tiny preview theatre in London's Soho that early autumn, desperately wanting to be as scared shitless as our gobsmacked brethren across the water.

Some might have been, but speaking personally I'd never felt more let down. I'm paraphrasing my two-page *Starburst* review at the time but I called it "puffed up beyond all logic or sense, borderline dull, isn't in the least bit scary, appropriates the narrative device used to much more devastating effect in *Cannibal Holocaust*, deliberately artless mockumentary, the biggest con trick of the year, redundant fantasy, even Ed Wood wrote better plots, I was restless and bored because nothing happens". And that was just for starters...

Nor have I changed my opinion over a movie that might have stood Hollywood Horror on its head but was very much lightning in a bottle and a product of its naïve online fake news time. Interesting that Adam Wingard's *Blair Witch* remake tanked for using similar outdated tricks like the ridiculous critical over-praising. Why did they think they could get away with it again?

Those who waxed-lyrical over *The Blair Witch Project* barely gave the hasty sequel *Book of Shadows: Blair Witch 2* the time of day. Yet the only way was up for me. For like Wes Craven's *Scream* franchise, with *Book of Shadows* proper documentary filmmaker Joe Berlinger at least attempted to explore the relationship between horror movies and their core audience while trying to pay homage to the first film. It was a stock deconstruction in the final analysis but at least it delivered the gory goods rather than a few giblets in a Kleenex!

I doubt whether there's any more gold in them thar Black Hills, but it wouldn't surprise me to see someone with more money that common sense try. Ask me to recall anything specific from the original film and I can't – apart from the giblet disappointment. But ask me my favourite memory and that's easy. I had to interview Linda Blair, star of *The Exorcist*, at a Manhattan Fangoria convention in 2000 and she gave me a copy of her latest straight-to-video release, the twenty minute short *The Blair Bitch Project* (Scott LaRose). Now that Jerkittsville-set spoof was funny!

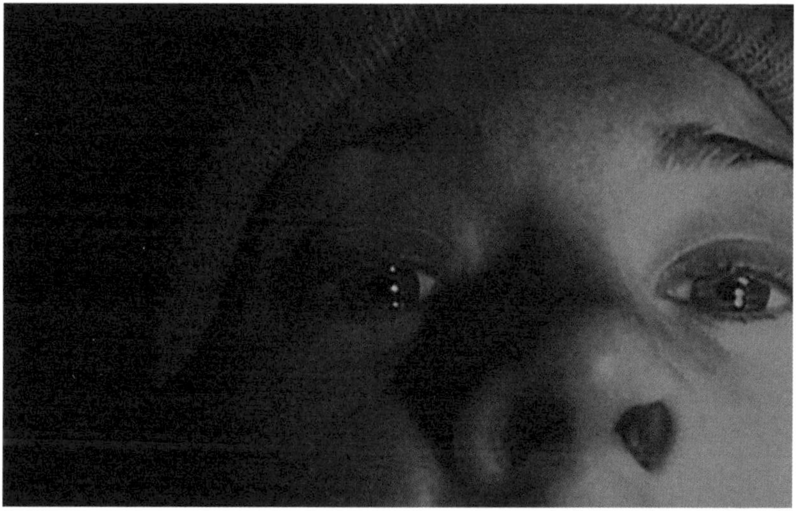

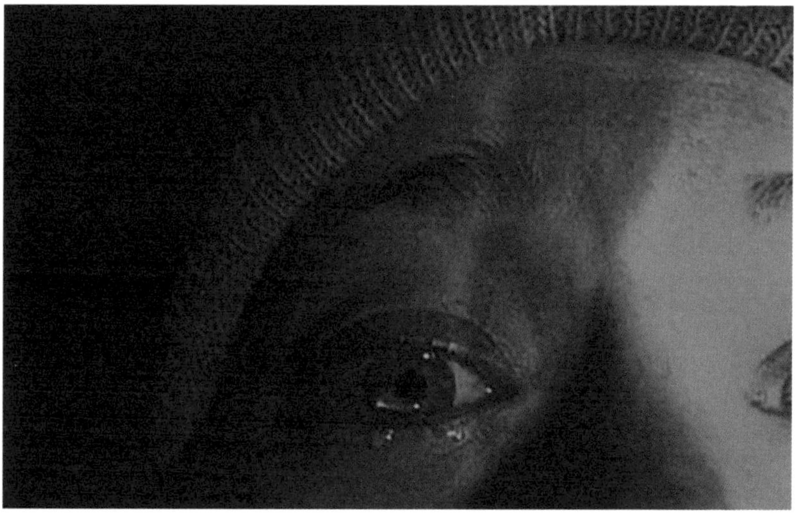

# Chapter Eleven

## A year later their footage was found

After the success of *The Blair Witch Project* the Haxan Films team had set up their basecamp in Orlando and begun working on various TV projects and the next film that Ed and Dan would direct – a comedy in the vein of *Airplane!* (Jim Abrahams, David Zucker & Jerry Zucker, 1980) with *Monty Python*-esque undertones.

*Heart of Love* was a comedy concept that the two filmmakers came up with shortly after making their debut. They wanted to do a complete 180° on the whole horror scene and go straight into a whacky comedy feature. A long time was spent on development and a script was finished. An animatic was even drafted for production. Unfortunately, as is so often the case, the full budget could not be raised and the project languished.

Haxan Films were still taking a break from horror, but Artisan Entertainment had other ideas. In a bid to recreate the box office success of the original film, the studio set a sequel release date of Halloween 2000 – far too tight a turnaround for the original creators to be involved with the production.

However, Haxan Films weren't completely done with the *Blair Witch* yet.

After considering possible ideas for a new *Blair Witch* film that would fit well in the universe they had created, in particular a prequel, Rob recommended that Ben put together (and be in charge of) the '*Blair Witch Black Bible*', which contained every single detail necessary on the first film and the legend. TV network Showtime was preparing to have the cable premiere of *The Blair Witch Project* in the summer and they wanted a TV special similar to *Curse of the Blair Witch*. Artisan also showed interest in creating a new special to help promote their upcoming sequel *Book of Shadows: Blair Witch 2* (Joe Berlinger, 2000). Upon recommendation from Gregg, Artisan hired Ben to write and direct these two documentaries. The first, *The Burkittsville 7* (Ben Rock, 2000), looks at the legend of the *Blair Witch* in an attempt to uncover the truth regarding the Rustin Parr killings in the 1940s. Following this, *Shadow of the Blair Witch* (Ben Rock, 2000) investigated the crime spree that was the supposed inspiration for *Book of Shadows*.

Ben called in his friend and fellow *Blair Witch* team-mate Neal Fredericks to work as cinematographer on both of the specials. They were produced back-to-back while production on *Book of Shadows* was well underway in Baltimore, Maryland.

I can't remember where the line between the hype for *The Blair Witch Project* ended and the excitement for *Book of Shadows* began. I have been trying to think back to when I first realised there was going to be sequel and I can't put my finger on it. I do however remember sometime in 2000 seeing a creepy poster with a stickman-symbol-bloodstain on a brown background. There was no real information on the poster except at the bottom, where it simply said "BW2 – October 27 – blairwitch.com". I don't remember going to the site again or even trying to find out much about the film, I was just taken by the eye candy of the poster and awaited trailers and the cinema release.

*Book of Shadows* was a controversial sequel. There is much information floating around on the World Wide Web (and also on the DVD Commentary) which details the disagreements and tension between the studio and director Joe Berlinger.

Joe Berlinger had created a career for himself in documentaries with his filmmaking partner, Bruce Sinofsky. The films that the pair made looked at real life murders in a unique and cinematic way. Joe had been looking for a way to break out of the documentary business, in which he felt trapped, so when Artisan called for him to pitch a feature film, he seized the opportunity.

Joe knew he would have one chance to make headlines when moving from documentaries to feature films and wanted to pick the perfect project – a noir thriller called *The Little Fellow in the Attic*, which was a true-crime story. After several increasingly important pitches to executives at Artisan, Joe realised they weren't interested in his film idea but were actually testing the water with him to see if he would be a good choice to direct their sequel *Blair Witch 2*.

The attention was flattering and Joe signed on to direct. He soon realised that Artisan wanted to continue the story from the first film, using the same found footage style. He was given the choice of three scripts – none of which he liked – and was to begin shooting in February 2000, just a matter of weeks away. Joe decided to pass, stating that it was a huge mistake to try and recapture the first film. Artisan took note of this and gave the option for Joe to pitch and write his own script examining the hysteria that the first film had caused. Joe co-wrote the screenplay for *Book of Shadows* in six weeks with Dick Beebe, who had previously written *House on Haunted Hill* (William Malone, 1999). Filming was soon underway and all seemed well.

In May and June 2000, early cuts of the film were screened and approved by Artisan. However, by the time Joe had turned in his director's cut of the film, a new marketing executive had been brought on board who ultimately decided that even though the film was scheduled for release in two months, rather than the edgy adult satire that had been delivered, they wanted a gory teen-slasher movie instead.

Changes were made and the tone of the film was altered from what Joe had originally envisaged. Editing continued right up to the last minute, with new footage being shot as close as five weeks before the theatrical release. The film was supposed to be ambiguous, serving as both a traditional horror film and also a satirical look at the effects of violence in the media. It was also a social commentary about the dangers of blurring the lines between fiction and reality. Originally the first half of *Book of Shadows* would have been more tongue-in-cheek before delving into pure horror. Evidently Artisan were expecting another found footage film but, coming from a background of documentary filmmaking, Joe just wasn't comfortable with the dishonesty of making a fake documentary.

*Book of Shadows* was made for around $15 million and despite earning $47 million worldwide it is still deemed a box office failure. The reviews were bad, targeting both the film and Joe Berlinger personally. Unfortunately Joe never has yet to make another Hollywood feature film. As a sequel to *The Blair Witch Project*, the film wasn't a success. However, as a horror film in its own right, *Book of Shadows* more than delivered, blending cinematic style and human emotion with a horrific sense of dread. It was the fact that the film didn't follow the same path as its predecessor that made it so polarising.

I was very happy that *Book of Shadows* was not another found footage film – especially (as we didn't know then) since the market place was about to become flooded with a mass of movies trying to capitalise on the success of the original. The reason most of these found footage films have failed is largely because they didn't capture a sense of dread and reality and also because they didn't actually bother to look at why *The Blair Witch Project* worked so well – both the marketing and mythology. It doesn't do just to run around the woods with a camera filming things that might be scary. There is so much more to it than that.

The term "found footage" is often misused. Most of the films that wish to adhere to this label do so incorrectly. Many are in fact "first-person", especially when the footage isn't explicitly found (as it was in the *Blair* mythology). I mean seriously, how many filmmakers out there are really losing all their footage?

There have been some hugely successful films in this style over the years but it wasn't until nearly ten years later when things got a fresh coat of paint with the release of *Paranormal Activity* (Oren Peli, 2007). This film managed to do what most of the others couldn't: it got a huge media buzz before it was released and again blurred the lines between fact and fiction for audiences. No one knew if it was real. It seemed real. It seemed possible. It was fucking terrifying. *Paranormal Activity* was clever with its technique and the marketing was perfect. Audiences lapped it up, so much so that between 2010 and 2015 there were five sequels – not including *Paranormal Activity: Tokyo Night* (Toshikazu Nagae, 2010). None of the sequels were quite as popular as the first film. This is not to say that they were bad; lightning just doesn't strike twice.

*The Blair Witch Project* itself was just so unique that there was no possible way to replicate it, no matter how hard the studios may try.

# The Blair Witch Experience

## Joe Berlinger

*Academy Award-nominated filmmaker Joe Berlinger has been a leading voice in non-fiction film and television for two decades. Berlinger's films with Bruce Sinofsky include the landmark documentaries* Brother's Keeper *(1992),* Paradise Lost *(1996), and* Metallica: Some Kind of Monster *(2004), a film that re-defined the rockumentary genre. In addition to his feature documentary work, Berlinger also directed the horror sequel* Book of Shadows: Blair Witch 2.

*The Blair Witch Project* was a unique cultural phenomenon. Whether or not they saw the movie, almost everyone around the globe heard the Cinderella-story of the little $30,000 film that became one of the most successful independent movies of all time. The film, both stylistically and through its marketing, brilliantly blurred the line between fact and fiction. As a documentarian, I was fascinated that many moviegoers left the film convinced that they had seen an actual documentary, or, at the very least, that the legend must be true. To me, *The Blair Witch Project* represented the confluence of several key ingredients: the use of the internet to market a fictitious story as fact; the public's active search for alternatives to standard Hollywood entertainment; and the widespread yearning, at the end of the 20th century, for proof that the paranormal/supernatural exists in our very scientific, unspiritual world. It was a case of the right film at the right time, propelled by a new medium – the internet. Because of the singular circumstances attending the film and its success, I thought a different kind of sequel – one that defies expectations – could be created.

The traditional choice for a sequel would have been to continue the story where the first movie left off. Because *The Blair Witch Project* was presented as a documentary, I thought it would be too much to ask audiences to once again suspend disbelief and accept that Heather, Josh and Mike were real students who actually were missing. After all, we all saw them on the covers of Time and Newsweek and on the David Letterman show. A more interesting approach would be to acknowledge the success of *The Blair Witch Project* and the worldwide cultural phenomenon that it precipitated – and then turn that idea on its head. By making a sequel about the impact of the first movie through five characters who are obsessed with it, I hoped to create a psychological horror movie that served a mainstream audience while simultaneously commenting on the media-created event that was the *Blair Witch*, thus connecting my first narrative feature with the kind of social analysis I have undertaken in my documentary work.

I chose to abandon the production techniques that were a key factor in the first movie's success – an ironic decision since I am best known for cinéma-vérité explorations of backwoods America in *Brother's Keeper* and the *Paradise Lost* documentaries. It was my belief that one does not have to rely on production technique to create an emotionally truthful cinematic experience. The faux documentary conceit worked wonderfully in the first film, but to revisit that approach would have been derivative and creatively unexciting – both for moviegoers and myself. Although I made use of mixed media (digital video, Hi-8 video, 16mm, computer graphics), *Book of Shadows* was primarily a 35mm film that used the traditional tools of motion picture production, and reflected a conscious directorial decision to evoke classic horror movies in its look and feel.

*Book of Shadows* defied expectations with the very central dramatic question that propelled the narrative: are the five main characters the latest victims of the evil that resides in the Black Hills, or is it possible that the Blair Witch does not exist at all? Could our five obsessed Blair Witch groupies have gone on a killing spree not because of a "witch" but because of mass hysteria seeded by the media frenzy surrounding *The Blair Witch Project*?

In many ways *Book of Shadows* was a post-modern sequel.

The original movie was extremely effective in portraying the devolving psychological state of three characters in a predicament beyond their control. This psychological unravelling of characters, and the sense of inevitability that surrounded their fate, was to me one of its greatest achievements and something I wanted to bring to the second film. I also wanted to explore a consistent theme from my documentary work – that evil is human, not supernatural; that it comes from within, not from without. To me, what is truly scary is not some inexplicable supernatural force, but rather human action. Evil is what humans are capable of doing to each other – and then not remembering. I thought one way to approach the sequel would be to tell a story about five kids who don't remember what they did and may in fact be responsible for acts of unspeakable evil.

My aim was that people would see *Book of Shadows* as a meditation on violence in the media and how the media shapes an event. I want viewers to ask: does media violence alone inspire real-life violence, or is that as simplistic and naive as blaming the Blair Witch? I hope the film does what I have always endeavoured to do in my work: examine complex subjects with the respect and thought they deserve. I like to raise issues and present both sides, but not necessarily answer all of the questions.

# Chapter Twelve

## The aftermath

*Book of Shadows* came and went and fans had collected almost every item of *Blair Witch* merchandise possible – from comic books to video games, figures to expanded universe novels and everything in between. Horror heads grew busy with their excitement for upcoming films such as *Jeepers Creepers* (Victor Salva, 2001), *Cabin Fever* (Eli Roth, 2002) and *Wrong Turn* (Rob Schmidt, 2003) and before long the terror of *The Blair Witch Project* was forgotten.

Fans still hoped for a third instalment of the film, but it seemed less and less likely. The fact that *Book of Shadows* came out one year after the first film and then there was silence didn't give much hope for more cinematic misadventures in the woods.

In the back of one of the *Blair Witch Files* novels was a teasing advert for a contest asking readers to tell of their brush with the supernatural in 150 words or fewer for a chance to win an all-expenses-paid trip to the set of *Blair Witch 3*. I wonder how many poor saps entered this competition. I wonder if there was a winner…

The unfortunate dissolution of *Heart of Love* and lack of creative involvement in *Book of Shadows* led the team at Haxan Films to move on with new projects which took them further away from their humble beginnings. After their success they were highly sought after and their next project was to be a series which aired on Fox called *Freakylinks* (2000–2001) and developed a cult following.

In 2004 Gregg made his feature film debut as director with the romantic comedy drama *Say Yes Quickly* (2004). By this time Ed had settled in Maryland while Dan moved to Los Angeles. Work began on a project that Dan was directing called *The Strand* (2007). The film was independently financed and shot in and around Venice Beach, detailing the lives and exploits of several interrelated characters that live in that area. It was all fictional, but shot very much with a documentary-style vibe. Ed visited the production to lend a hand as a camera operator.[7]

Ed was taking some time out to decide on his next project when a script from writer Jamie Nash found its way to him. The two of them then worked on the screenplay for *Probed* together before taking it to Gregg and Rob to produce. This fun little alien horror film was released with the new title *Altered* (2006) and starred Mike Williams from *The Blair Witch Project*. Tony Cora also returned to create an incredible score for the film.

Dan started a new label – Raw Feed – and produced several films including his own *Believers* (2007) and Ben's feature debut *Alien Raiders* (2008). Dan continued directing with *Solstice* (2008) and *The Objective* (2008), which also starred Mike Williams. Meanwhile Ed and Gregg travelled to China to film *Seventh Moon* (Eduardo Sanchez, 2008) from a script by Ed and Jamie Nash. Tony once again provided the score and Rob produced.

During this time Ed and Dan still had thoughts of revisiting the *Blair Witch*. Several sequel concepts and a prequel idea were worked on. The pair co-wrote a very unique script for Lionsgate which would serve as a terrifying sequel but unfortunately the film never went into production.

I visited Hagerstown, Maryland in October 2010 to work filming Transmedia[8] and behind-the-scenes for *Lovely Molly* (Eduardo Sanchez, 2011) – an absolutely terrifying film that didn't get as big a release as it deserved. Jamie and Ed wrote the film, Gregg and Rob produced. I got my chance to visit Burkittsville during the shoot as two of my friends from the crew and I drove out there to look around. It was eerie seeing locations from *The Blair Witch Project*, such as the graveyard. Funnily enough an Asian family also "sightseeing" saw us and asked, in all honesty, if we knew where the Blair Witch was buried. Not being able to resist I enhanced their trip by explaining that according to legend Elly Kedward, the Witch, had not been buried here but was left to die out in the woods.

---

7 The Strand can be seen (with a bunch of behind-the-scenes footage) at www.strandvenice.com.

8 Transmedia is the creation of additional content in order to share a single story experience across multiple platforms, which in turn creates a deeper narrative universe.

I pointed out to the nearest woods and left them to think about it. I worked again with Ed in 2013 when I edited the web series *Four Corners of Fear* (Eduardo Sanchez, 2013). Fans of *The Blair Witch Project* enjoyed the series as it was released very teasingly as a follow up to the film, but turned out to be a spoof showing the making of a very unusual BW3.

Ed and Gregg revisited found footage when they co-directed the segment *A Ride in the Park* for the horror anthology *V/H/S 2* (Various Directors, 2013) and then dug deep into their childhood fears to bring Bigfoot back to the screens in *Exists* (Eduardo Sanchez, 2014), both written with Jamie Nash.

Horror fans waited and waited for another trip to Burkittsville. There were teases online that Lionsgate (who owned the theatrical Halloween slot with the *Saw* franchise) might look to revisit the *Blair Witch* as a new franchise. It wasn't until the middle of 2016 that a creepy trailer appeared for a new film called *The Woods* (Adam Wingard, 2016) that audiences began to get excited for another film in the series. If you were to look carefully at that first trailer (and I mean frame by frame), there were at least two shots that showed stickmen hanging in the woods.

On July 22nd 2016 *The Woods* was to screen at San Diego Comic-Con and audiences were mostly unaware that the film they were seeing was actually titled *Blair Witch*. Upon exiting the cinema they soon realised that all of the posters and banners that bore the title The Woods had been replaced with the new title. It became clear to the world that director Adam Wingard and writer Simon Barrett had been secretly working with Lionsgate to revisit the Black Hills woods in a direct sequel to *The Blair Witch Project*, with the desire and passion to continue the legend created by the small team at Haxan Films nearly twenty years previously.

This incredible marketing strategy worked and gave audiences a sense of excitement and fear. No longer could you trick people into thinking a film was real, but you could divert their attention and create a huge impact that way instead.

This was proof indeed that there was still life left in Elly Kedward yet.

The Witch had returned!

# Dedication To Neal Fredericks (1969–2004)

## Ben Rock

I remember Neal's funeral in 2004 like I'm still there. It was late in the summer and there were a bunch of us, mostly in our thirties, blankly staring at Neal's coffin as if it couldn't be. For most of us, he was our first friend to die. Early adulthood felt like an extended adolescence (especially in L.A. where everything is about youth) and an artefact of that is the sense that everyone is immortal or at least that everyone has decades and decades to know each other, to work with each other.

I'm sure that as Red Hot Chili Peppers' 'Scar Tissue' played in its entirety at the beginning of Neal's memorial service, most of us were thinking about how he'd just been there. Just a few weeks earlier Alicia (to whom I'm now married), Matt Compton and I had seen him off to the production he was shooting in the Florida Keys. A few weeks before that I'd edited his DP reel in Final Cut Pro in the same room where I now write this. If I turn to my right I can see the chair where he sat that day.

I'd met Neal many times in film school, but I really met Neal the day he showed up in October of 1997 to DP *The Blair Witch Project*. He had probably the driest sense of humour of anyone I'd ever met. He'd often test you by saying something outrageous with a deadpan straight face and when he saw that gleam of "Are you serious?" in your eye he'd look down with the ghost of a smile and shake his head to let you know you'd been had. If you meet Ed Sanchez, to this day, he has that mannerism, purloined from Neal. I liked him immediately and hoped he liked me. When I got lost in the woods one day and wandered to a phone about a mile from where we'd all been, I called Neal and he picked me up. I was expecting him to make merciless fun of me and my poor ground navigation skills, but he never mentioned it to anyone as far as I know.

I didn't see Neal again after the *Blair Witch* shoot until the day in early January 1999 when I arrived in L.A. and, by coincidence, it was the same day the film had been picked up for distribution by Artisan Entertainment. After having driven across the country, Alicia and I picked Neal up in LA – a city we didn't yet know and Alicia and Neal had not previously met – and we drove twelve hours to Park City, Utah, together. From that moment onward, he was one of my best friends in LA; the guy who'd call me up to see if I wanted to join him for the horror movie nobody but he and I would want to see. When I was offered my first opportunity to direct professionally, the only DP I considered was him and he thanked me repeatedly for thinking of him for the job when I always felt that it was he doing me the favour by working with me – he was a lifeline the entire shoot. Neal loved shooting film for the art of it and the *esprit de corps* of working with and marshalling a crew. After calling "Cut," I'd ask him: "How did that look?" and he'd say, "Fucking sweet!" And he meant it. He treated his camera and lighting crew like superstars and had no problem pushing back against producers who treated them poorly.

Those of us who knew him still think of Neal often and tell his story – although for me it's usually in the context of why on any set I don't fuck around with safety (and I do not fuck around with safety). I flatter myself to say that if he were still around today, I hope we'd still be collaborating on this or that, nerding out on cameras or editing gear, picking apart grotesque horror movies. I know above all we'd still be friends and I assume he'd be shooting giant movies by now. Shooting movies was his calling, his art, his passion. The day after his funeral I was set to direct a forty-eight hour film project and grief-stricken I thought about not doing it, but then I thought about what Neal would want me to do and I knew that I had to shoot. We dedicated the film to him, a flimsy tribute but the best I was able to muster at the time.

**The Blair Witch Project**

**USA 1999**

1 hr 21 min (81min)
Dolby SR
Black and White / Color
1.33:1

**Camera**
Cinema Products CP-16A
RCA Hi-8 Camcorder
**Format**
Eastman Double-X 7222 16mm Film
Hi-8 Video Tape
**Printed Film Format**
35mm

**Directors**
Daniel Myrick and Eduardo Sanchez
**Producers**
Gregg Hale and Robin Cowie
**Co-Producer**
Michael Monello
**Executive Producers**
Bob Eick and Kevin J. Foxe
**Screenplay**
Daniel Myrick and Eduardo Sanchez
**Edited by**
Daniel Myrick and Eduardo Sanchez
**Production Designer**
Ben Rock
**Art Director**
Ricardo R. Moreno

**Director of Photography**
Neal Fredericks
**Music Composer**
Tony Cora

**Phase One Instigators**
John Pierson – Grainy Pictures
Howard Bernstien
**Additional Photography**
Hector Lopez
**Processing By**
Colorlab
**Video to Film Transform**
4MC
David Donaldson
Beverly Brooks
**Music Assistant**
Dan Barrio
**Sound Mix**
Dana Meeks
**Audition Assistants**
Matt Compton
Stefanie DeCassan
Carolyn DeCassan
Fahad Vania
Britt Nichols
Rachel Carter
Kelly Phipps
**Additional Casting**
Lisa Lane
**Final Mix**
Wilshire Stages
Gerry Lentz, CAS
Rich Weingart

Harry Cohen, MPSE

**Accounting**

Sarah Cowie

Gene O'Baker

Wolf, Young, O'Baker

Shelley Buell

**Marketing**

Harry Clein

Jeremy Walker

Clein + Walker

**Audio**

Jack Sherdel

and the entire staff at Digitec

**Locations**

Matt Compton

Melvin Bayer

Adamstown Village Market

B.B. Browns Lawn and Garden

Christian Gueverra

RDV Sports

Silver Rail Diner

Staub's Country Inn

The St Augustine Old Jail

WESH Channel 2, Orlando, FL

**Legal**

Bill Whitacre

**Investor Tape Production**

Joe Solari

Wendy Smith

Dave Segal

Trey Butts

Dennis Warner

Crystal Jordan

Jenn Winn

**Still Photography**

Stefanie DeCassan

Julie Ann Smith

**Scenic Art**

Andrew White

Brigan Docking

**Art Technician**

Patricia DeCou

**Stunt Rigging**

Douglas Retzler

Steven A. Blake

**Behind-The-Scenes Video**

Zubi Mohammed

Ray Combs

**Key PA**

Lonnie Glerum

**Production Assistants**

Stefanie DeCassan

Carolyn DeCassan

Julia Fair

Shannon Kibler

Kurt McNew

Tina Plank

Billy Plank

Dave Poole

Sandra Sanchez

Adrian Steinbach

Fahad Vania

Mark Bobrow

**Special Thanks**

Jane E. Barrick

Teresa Bone

Peter Broderick

Carmen Cacaven

Larry Carneglia
Brian Clark
Sandy Craig
Matthew Curtis
Dex Dean – Coastal Leasing
Cecilia DeCassan
Gina DeCassan
Enzian Theater
FILMMAKER Magazine
Sarah Foxe
Richard and Ingrid Fraley
Melanie Gasper
Ellen Gillis
Lonnie Glerum
Greta – Christensen Group
Christian Guevara
Dee Guzzi
Tonya Hale
Lynda Hansen
Thomas Ethan Harris
Hudson Trails Outfitters
Diana Iwanow
Jeff Johnson
Mary Johnson
Bob Jones
Mike Jones
Nancy King
Lousie Levinson
Jean Lipphard
Sandra Lukas
Mark & Brian Show
Terry Martin
Margarita Moreno
Oscar Moreno
Dick Morris
Mott's Fruit Punch
Joe Nagy
Michael Nelson
Peg O'Keef
Anthony Pekarik
Klark J. Perez
John Pierson
Janet Pierson
Power Bar, Inc.
Don Rhodes
Rio Grande
Brian Saway
Cecilia Saway
Rick Saway
William Saway
Catherine Smith
Don Smith
Stackpole Books
Success Rice
Susanne Haley Talent
University of Central Florida
Vaughn Broadcast Rental
Dennis Warner
Paul K. Williamson
St Augustine Amphitheatre
Lorraine Wood
Tara Zwicker

**Extra Special Thanks**

Stefanie DeCassan
Richard and Jan Ungaro
Lindsey and Francis Tanner
Gene O'Baker
Steve Boudreau

Scott Macquarrie
Karol Cavanaugh
Jack Sherdel
Dave Norman
Kurt McNew
Jim and Korrin Ritzel
Jackie Hale
Les and Fran Cowie
Ali Steinbach

**Cast**
Heather Donahue
Joshua Leonard
Michael Williams
With
Bob Griffin
Jim King
Sandra Sanchez
Ed Swanson
Patricia DeCou
Mark Mason
Jackie Hallex

"Rigors" by Klaus Heesch.
Performed by Digginlilies.
Courtesy of Juicy Temples

"The Ballad of Gilligan's Isle
(Theme from Gilligan's Island)".
By George Wyle and Sherwood Schwartz.
Courtesy of EMI U Catalog Inc.

"How to Stay Alive in the Woods"
Used by permission of Curtis Brown Ltd.

Shot on location in Seneca Creek and
Patapsco Valley State Parks
Courtesy Maryland Department of Natural Resources

Posted on the Media 100XR at
Haxan Films, Orlando, Florida

Motion Picture Association of America
#36716

Released by Artisan Entertainment

# About The Author

Russ Gomm is a filmmaker with an undying love of horror films and *Star Wars*. He was drawn into the strange world of cinema after watching such genre fare as *Return of the Jedi* (Richard Marquand, 1983), *Blade Runner* (Ridley Scott, 1982) and *Mad Max* (George Miller, 1979), all by the age of seven. His recent films include the features *The Woods Movie* (2015) and *The Legend of the Mad Axeman* (2017) and the short *The Welcoming* (2017). A love of mythology bought *The Blair Witch Project* to his attention in 1999 and he has been recovering ever since. It was inevitable that he would be the one to write this book.

# Acknowledgements

Firstly, thanks to everyone who contributed to this book:
Eduardo Sanchez, Daniel Myrick, Ben Rock, Jake West, Garland Triest, Johannes Roberts, Mitch Harrod, Sean Plummer, Joe Lynch, Matt Blazi, Dave Stern, Alan Jones and Joe Berlinger. This book has been enriched with your incredible insights and experiences.

I would also like to praise every member of the amazing team behind *The Blair Witch Project* for all of their hard work in producing such a horrifying and thought-provoking film. Fans and filmmakers will appreciate this horror gem for many more years to come.

Thank you Gregg Hale and Robin Cowie for making me feel like part of the Haxan family.

Thanks to everyone at Arrow Films (especially Mike Hewitt and Kevin Lambert) for giving me the chance to share my passion and experience of *The Blair Witch Project*.

Thanks to Jenai Laignel for being a really fabulous editor.

Thank you Jamie Nash, Lin Fahrenheit, Matthew Nagy, Joe Nagy, Stefanie Sanchez, Ken Arnold, Dan Karcher, Jacob Sanders, Tony Cora, Zubi Mohammed, Wayne Mitchell, John Simmonds, Jonathan Olliver, Philip Mearns, Jack Tapley, Colin & Sylvi Marman, Barry Twyman, Barry & Victoria Blackburn, Jean-Paul & Rebecca Muller, Mark, Val, Adam & Sarah Modley. Thanks to Sean, Marlene, Dani, Dave, Dillon, John, Alexis, Caleb, Reuben, Paul and Siobhan, and big thanks to all of my friends who have spent countless hours listening to me continuously talk about *The Blair Witch Project*, over and over again.

And most importantly, thank you Mum, Dad, Dominic, Lorraine and Connor for your constant support, and putting up with all the hours spent creating this book.

This book is dedicated to everyone who has ever gone out to make an independent film, no matter how big or small, and can truly appreciate how much hard work goes into it.